KU-471-600

Contents

Preface

This text is intended primarily for those students of accountancy who wish to learn something of the subject's management dimension. It assumes only a very basic knowledge of financial and cost accounting, and should therefore be suitable as an introductory text.

Throughout, the use of language has been kept uncomplicated in order to assist the student whose mother tongue is not English.

PP 8909064 0

YORK BUSINESS HANDBOOKS

GENERAL EDITOR:
Sir Kenneth Alexander

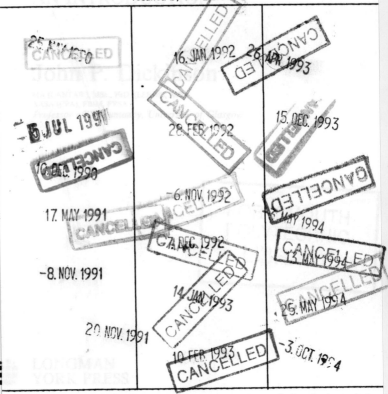

PORTSMOUTH POLYTECHNIC LIBRARY

CLASS NUMBER 658.1511 OIC

LOCATION

To be returned by the last date or time stamped below, or when
recalled by the Librarian.

Loans remain the responsbility of the borrower until cancelled at the loans desk

8909064

To Anthony

YORK PRESS
Immeuble Esseily, Place Riad Solh, Beirut.

LONGMAN GROUP UK LIMITED
Longman House,
Burnt Mill,
Harlow,
Essex.

© Librairie du Liban 1987

*All rights reserved. No part of this publication may be reproduced,
stored in a retrieval system, or transmitted in any form or by any
means, electronic, mechanical, photocopying, recording, or otherwise,
without the prior permission of the copyright owner.*

First published 1987
ISBN 0 582 00348 2
Printed in Singapore

Acknowledgements

My sincere thanks are due to Elissa and Elspeth for their invaluable assistance in preparing the manuscript, and for bearing innumerable amendments with remarkable equanimity.

Apologies are due to Christine, Rachel, Vanessa, and Anthony who – with exemplary tolerance – have seen a quiet sabbatical transformed into turmoil.

J. P. DICKINSON

Bridge of Allan
June 1986

List of Figures

Chapter 1

Development and rôle of accounting

1.1 Introduction

Accountancy as a profession began with the development of double-entry book-keeping several centuries ago. At that time, increasing commercial activity within and between trading nations demanded an objective system for keeping financial records. Early business organisations were based largely upon families or partnerships with little need to report widely to the outside world. However, this changed with the creation of limited liability companies in which members of the public at large could buy shares. As part-owners, shareholders have an interest in – and a right to – information concerning the financial state and progress of a company. In addition, such information is needed by Government for taxation purposes, by financial institutions such as banks, and by employees.

Reporting on the financial aspects of an organisation to interested parties outside it is known as *financial accounting*. The major rôle of the *financial accountant* is that of stewardship, i.e. preparing financial reports which give information about how the organisation has used its assets to those, for example, who have provided the funds used to purchase the assets. The two major reports which have been prepared by the financial accountant for outside users are the *balance sheet* and the *profit and loss account* (or *income statement*). The interrelationship between these and the *statement of accumulated profit* is shown in Fig. 1.

It is important to note that the traditional activities of the financial accountant relate to financial events which have already happened. He is concerned with reporting *historical costs* which have been incurred, and which therefore may have little use in planning or controlling the future progress of the organisation. Financial accounting has the added limitation that it deals with the organisation overall, and not at a detailed level. A simple analogy compares the business organisation with a car. The financial accounts provide a photograph of the car, and a description of where it has come from. They give, however, no guidance as to where the car might go in the future, nor how the various components within the car should be operated to get there.

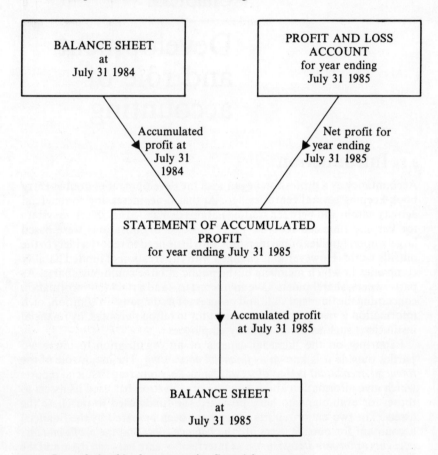

FIG. 1: **Interrelationships between major financial statements**

1.2 Cost accounting

Within the organisation many financial events take place each day. These include payment of wages and salaries, purchase of raw materials, and the sale of finished goods. At a detailed level they are of interest to neither the world outside the organisation nor the financial accountant. Nevertheless, they are obviously of great importance to the continuing operation of the organisation. The particular branch of accounting which was developed to record and analyse the internal financial aspects of an organisation is known as *cost accountancy*. Traditionally, the rôle of the cost accountant has centred on matters such as:

(i)   estimation of cost of unfinished goods (work-in-progress) and finished goods, and

(ii) estimation of cost per unit of product manufactured.

At any stage in a production process there are likely to be some products finished and awaiting sale, whilst others remain partially finished. Therefore (i) is important if profit for an accounting period is to be measured at the end of that period. Without the recording and channelling of all costs through to products, which is implied by (ii), it would not be possible to arrive at a selling price for the product which would be sure to cover all the costs. Very important though these objectives are, it is worth noting that the cost accountant, like the financial accountant, is here working with historic costs. Again, there is little scope for the planning and control of future operations.

1.3 Management accounting

Over relatively recent years, and with the increasing complexity, size, specialisation, and international nature of the modern business organisation the need has arisen for a new type of professional accountant. His responsibility is to provide detailed financial and cost data to management in a form suitable for *decision-making*, *planning*, and *control* purposes. The modern *management accountant* – to give him his proper title – has a key function to serve management in a way which neither the financial accountant nor the cost accountant can do.

Planning, control, and decision-making functions are, of course, meaningless without an objective in mind. Recalling the earlier analogy, there is little point in driving a car if we do not know where we are going. Unfortunately, in a complex social and economic environment, it is often difficult for any individual or team to define clear goals for an organisation. Top management – whose responsibility it is – may be more concerned with survival in the short and medium term, and with the need to make a profit, not a loss. Obviously, in the absence of clear goals beyond survival and satisficing*, the management accountant's task becomes more difficult; he cannot advise management, or even identify management's information needs.

In understanding the importance of the management accountant, it might be helpful to consider the skills which he must have in order to perform his duties effectively. His main focus on decision-making, planning, and control requires a much wider knowledge than simply that of cost accounting. The planning aspect alone implies that he must have an

*See p. 137

awareness of the economic and social factors outside the firm – and their likely future trends – if he is to understand the market for the company's products. He must also have an appreciation of the markets from which the company draws its labour and raw materials. Control within the organisation implies a knowledge not only of technical matters involving the production process, but also of personnel management and industrial relations. His rôle in decision-making demands an understanding of behavioural factors, of statistical analysis, of operational research, and of computing. Finally – and crucially – for all three strands of his task he needs to be able to communicate to all levels of management. This may involve the transmission of agreed plans down to middle and lower management, the recommendation of plans to senior management, the feedback of information necessary for control when deviations from plan are detected, or the motivation of the workforce to achieve agreed plans.

Obviously no single person can be master of all the facets to the management accountant's job which have been mentioned. Nevertheless, some knowledge of all is necessary if he is to liaise effectively with, say, the managerial economist, the industrial psychologist, the systems analyst and so on. In other words, he needs to know when and to whom to turn for specialist advice, and he needs to be able to judge that advice intelligently.

The demands placed upon the accounting profession will no doubt continue to change in the future. An obvious recent development stems from advances in information technology, with particular impact on the accountant at the core of whose work information processing lies. Certainly the traditional accountant's preserves of tax accounting, auditing, and book-keeping have been much affected. Indeed, any area of the accountant's work which involves standard procedures and the application of a logical sequence of prescribed operations, is likely to shift to the computer. Even routine control operations involving corrective feedback action are, at a basic level, capable of being taken out of the accountant's hands. However, we must remember that the management accountant is not concerned solely with routine procedures. He is concerned also with future planning and control, and with decision-making. In all of these his judgement of the future, and his understanding of human behaviour are vital. It is possible that electronic aids may help the management accountant in meeting his responsibilities, but it is difficult to see how they can replace him.

Although cost accountants and management accountants have many similar interests it is important to understand and emphasise their differences. The cost accountant is concerned largely with recording, analysing, and classifying costs. The management accountant is concerned with using those historic, and future estimated, costs for management purposes. In this book the emphasis is on management accounting. For this reason administrative and cost recording procedures, which in any case may differ significantly between one company and another depending on size and degree of computerisation, are not considered in detail.

1.4 Nature of the manufacturing process

In order to understand more clearly the work and responsibilities of the management accountant, consider for a moment a typical manufacturing organisation. Its essential purpose is to make a product or products which can then be sold, to generate sales revenue. In order to manufacture the product resources are needed. These will include raw materials from which the products are made, labour, machinery and equipment, and factory facilities (plant). Additional support services such as transport, warehousing, administration, computing, and personnel will also be needed. If a continuing supply of manufactured goods for sale is to be maintained, all these resources must be available on a continuous or regular basis. Fig. 2 shows the organisation of a typical manufacturing process. In the figure input raw materials and labour are put together in the presence of *producing departments* (e.g. welding, machining, and finishing) and *service departments* in order to manufacture the product.

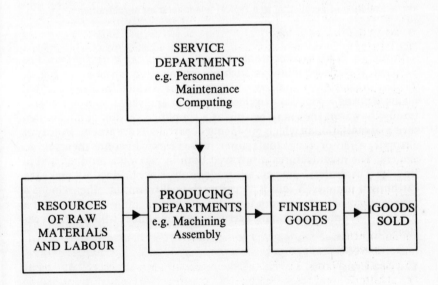

FIG. 2: **Production flow in a manufacturing organisation**

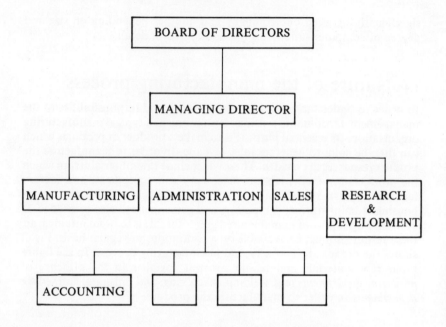

FIG. 3: **Location of accounting in a typical manufacturing organisation**

In this book we shall concentrate on *manufacturing organisations*. The location of the accountant in such an organisation is shown in Fig. 3. *Trading organisations* and *service organisations* – which involve no actual manufacturing – are also extremely common and very important. Structurally, however, they may be seen as a simplified version of a manufacturing organisation in which producing departments are absent. By way of example, a motor car manufacturer makes cars which are then sold to dealers. The manufacturer is involved both in making a product, and in trading. The dealer, however, is a trader only, since he does not make the car himself but merely sells it. A car-wash facility, on the other hand is a service organisation. It is not involved either in manufacture or sale of a product, but only in providing a service to the customer who wants his car cleaned.

Exercises

1. "Cost accounting is concerned solely with the collection, classification, and analysis of information." Discuss this statement.

2. "The management accountant must be able to communicate his findings effectively to all levels of management."

Discuss and explain the broad principles which you would follow in presenting reports to management.

3. "Management accounting is not a subject itself, but a mixture of statistics, behavioural science, costing, computing, and finance." Discuss.

Chapter 2

Costs: classification and flows

2.1 Introduction

Any systematic and objective approach to developing a body of knowledge requires clear definitions of the basic concepts involved. This not only allows the subject to be built in a logical manner, but also it aids unambiguous communication between individuals. The subjects of cost and management accounting are no exception to this general principle. The first few sections of this chapter therefore contain definitions of some fundamental terms which we will be using frequently. As the reader progresses through the book additional terms and their definitions will be introduced at appropriate stages.

A second major component of the scientific study of a subject involves classification. This has been applied very successfully, for example, in the physical sciences. Our understanding of the properties and structure of matter depends much upon the classification of substances into elements and compounds. In the life sciences too, understanding of evolution and animal behaviour owes a great deal to the classification of animal and plant life into families and species. In the social sciences the application of scientific methods has been less successful – at least so far. Partly this is due to the youth of the subject, and partly it is due to the difficulties of analysing and measuring human behaviour objectively. Accounting has some of the characteristics of a social science – since it deals with a human activity – and some of a physical science. As a result, parts of the subject can be treated in an objective, scientific, way and parts cannot. A detailed budget (see Chapter 8), for example, can be prepared step by step. Implementation of that budget may, however, require an understanding of individual and group behaviour which cannot be measured.

2.2 Definition of cost

The term *cost* is used in everyday language in a variety of ways. For example, we speak of the cost of a new car. We also might say that an accident in that car cost the driver his life. In the first case there are financial implications, in the second there are none (in the immediate sense, that is). Both examples, however, do involve a sacrifice – of money or of life.

Even in specialist language we find cost used in different senses. Thus an accountant usually refers to cost in relation to a completed transaction. An economist, however, might think of a cost in terms of an opportunity not taken. From an accountant's perspective the most satisfactory definition is one which recognises that an expenditure has been, or will be, made in order to obtain some economic benefit. Often this benefit secured will play a part in the generation of future revenue. Accordingly, we define cost as:

the amount of expenditure (i.e. a decrease in assets or an increase in liabilities) made in order to secure some goods or services.

Given the difficulties of arriving at a definition suitable for all purposes it is probably wise to avoid using the term "cost" on its own. Instead, it is helpful to qualify it with an additional word or words depending on the context. This is a practice which will be largely followed through this book.

A fundamental property of any cost in accounting is the ability it provides of comparing and contrasting very different concepts or objects. As a simple illustration, it is not possible to add together three hours of labour and two kilograms of raw materials. The wages and prices paid respectively for these two resources, however, provide a common yardstick for their comparison since both are measured in the same monetary units.

2.3 Cost classification

2.3.1 Bases for classification

In the following discussion various different classifications of cost will be introduced. It would be wrong to suggest that one criterion for classification is superior to the others. The fact of the matter is that all are important, and all are useful. Which classification is appropriate depends very much upon the particular circumstances of the organisation concerned, the nature of its product, and the purpose for which the costs are being analysed. Thus in one context, it may be useful to focus on whether a cost is direct or indirect. In another context it may be more appropriate to distinguish between fixed costs and variable costs. Classifications may overlap and a cost may, for example, be both a fixed cost and a period cost. An example would be building insurance.

2.3.2 Product costs and period costs

Some costs are identified naturally with products. They can be matched, in the period in which the product is sold, with the sales revenue generated by the sale. Such costs are known as *product costs*. If we are manufacturing cars the cost of the tyres would be an example of a product cost.

On the other hand, some costs are more readily assigned to periods of time rather than to products. Such costs are known as *period* costs, and are charged entirely against revenue in the accounting period during which the cost was incurred. As a simple illustration, central administration costs would normally be treated as a period cost.

The distinction between period and product costs is an important one when calculating income. This is discussed in detail in Chapter 6.

2.3.3 Functional classification

Bearing in mind the typical manufacturing process illustrated in Fig. 2 a natural means of classifying costs is by function. Thus we would refer to *production costs*, to *selling costs*, to *administration costs* and to *research and development costs*. Examples of these respectively might be, power consumption by machinery, salesmen's salaries, accountants' salaries, and attendance at a research conference.

2.3.4 Cost elements

Another approach to classification segregates costs under three headings: materials, labour, and expenses. The first of these relates to the costs of physical goods which either form part of the final product, or which are used up in the manufacturing process. The second is the costs which arise from employing people. The third category includes all costs which do not fall into either of the other two categories. The three categories are called the *cost elements*.

2.3.5 Direct and indirect costs

Some costs are incurred which can be traced in a natural way to a particular product, process, or department. These are known as *direct costs*.

However, it may be impossible – or too difficult or impractical – to trace a cost in this way. In that case the cost is referred to as an *indirect cost*.

The wages of the worker on a motor-car assembly line would be an example of a direct labour cost. The cost of the factory supervisor would probably be an indirect labour cost. It should be emphasised, however, that classification may not always be unambiguous.

2.3.6 Prime cost, conversion cost, and overhead

Indirect manufacturing costs (whether from materials, labour, or expenses) are normally collected together under the title of *manfacturing overhead* (or *factory overhead*).

Similarly, the result of aggregating all direct manufacturing costs (of materials, labour, and expenses) is referred to as the *prime cost*.

Sometimes the term *conversion cost* is used for the sum of direct labour costs and manufacturing overhead.

2.3.7 Fixed and variable costs

A final classification of costs is based upon their behaviour. It is found, not surprisingly, that in practice some costs vary with the volume of production activity, whilst others do not. More specifically, certain costs increase (or decrease) proportionately with increases (or decreases) in production activity. Such costs are called *variable costs*. By way of illustration suppose a motor-car factory assembles 200 cars per day. If production is increased by 10% to 220 cars per day, the cost of providing tyres for the vehicles will also increase by 10%. In this case, the cost of tyres is a variable cost.

On the other hand some costs, known as *fixed costs*, are found not to change over a range of different production levels. In the previous example, the salary of the factory supervisor and any factory rental charges would both be fixed costs, unaffected by the 10% increase in production. Although, as we shall see, the concept of fixed and variable costs can be extremely useful in budgeting and production planning, the classification needs to be treated with caution. For example, it could be that a 10% increase in production can be achieved only by renting further factory space, or by operating the production for a larger number of hours. In this case the rental or supervisory costs would increase, and could no longer be treated as fixed. The key factor to bear in mind is that the separation of costs into fixed and variable components is useful, but only over a limited range of possible production levels. Over a different, or wider, range the fixed cost base, and indeed the variable cost/unit, may change. A typical cost structure over a limited range is shown in Fig. 4, with other possible structures over much larger ranges of activity levels shown in Fig. 5.

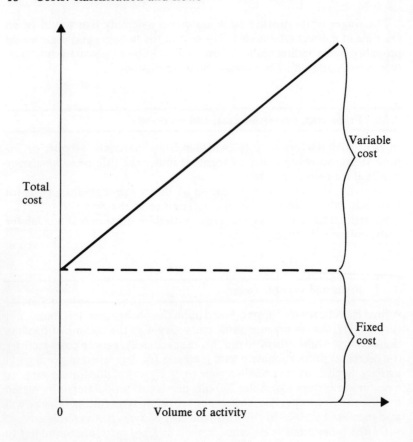

FIG. 4: **Fixed and variable costs**

It is quite common for a cost to be made up of a fixed component and a variable component. Total production cost, for example, may comprise a fixed production cost, and a variable production cost which is proportional to the number of units produced. Again, suppliers of power (e.g. electricity, gas) often charge a fixed sum, even if no power is used, plus a sum related to the number of units of power used. Thus, with a fixed charge of £5 for a period in which 500 kWh of electricity are used at a charge of 5p/kWh, the total cost would be £5 + 500 × 5p = £30. Such composite costs are called *semi-variable costs*.

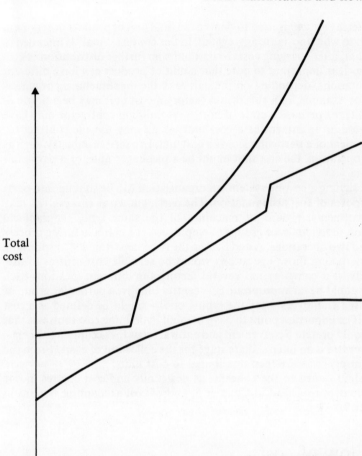

FIG. 5: **Some possible cost behaviours over wide ranges of activity level**

2.4 Cost centres and cost units

An important purpose in analysing and classifying costs is to enable them to be grouped, or *charged*, to different aspects of the organisation's activities. This in turn enables the eventual charging of costs to products, an objective referred to in §1.2.

The term *cost unit* is used to denote the final unit of product or service in relation to which costs are aggregated. In this context "final" is intended to mean that, after charging costs to cost units no further distribution of cost is made. It is important to note that a unit of product can have different interpretations, depending on the nature of the manufacturing organisation. For example, in a soft drinks factory a cost unit may be a bottle of lemonade, or perhaps a crate of bottles. A building contractor may have one house or apartment as a cost unit, or he may use the contract for development of a particular site as a cost unit. In a service industry, such as airline operation, the cost unit might be a passenger-mile, or a particular air-route.

In designing a costing system, an organisation can be split up into parts for purposes of cost accumulation. The parts, known as *cost centres*, may be departments, groups of machines of the same type, geographical locations, individuals, or groups of employees. If a manufacturing process involved two operations, A and B, then the two "departments" responsible for undertaking those operations would be sensible cost centres to use. Similarly, if a company has several factories in different locations each factory could be an appropriate cost centre. Finally, a particular group of specialised employees – say the typing pool – might be defined as a cost centre. The important point to have in mind in defining cost centres is that they should present a convenient and natural focus for accumulating costs. A cost centre is an intermediate stage for the collection of costs. From the cost centres, costs are then distributed to cost units.

We shall return to the concepts of cost units and cost centres in our discussions of overhead in Chapter 5, and of cost accounting systems in Chapter 7.

2.5 Flow of costs

The nature of a typical manufacturing process was illustrated in Fig. 2. It can be thought of in terms of a flow through the factory. Resources, including labour, are applied to raw materials inserted at the commencement of manufacturing. Gradually, as the raw materials pass from one stage to another they go through various stages of completion until eventually the finished product emerges.

In a similar way, it is helpful to think of cost flows. Although the pattern of such flows may follow the manufacturing process quite closely there are important differences. These arise because not all costs can be charged to cost units in a natural way, and because a major purpose of cost classification and accumulation is to trace the flow of costs into the profit and loss account (income statement). The general pattern of flows is shown in Fig. 6. Here it can be seen how costs are firstly separated into those

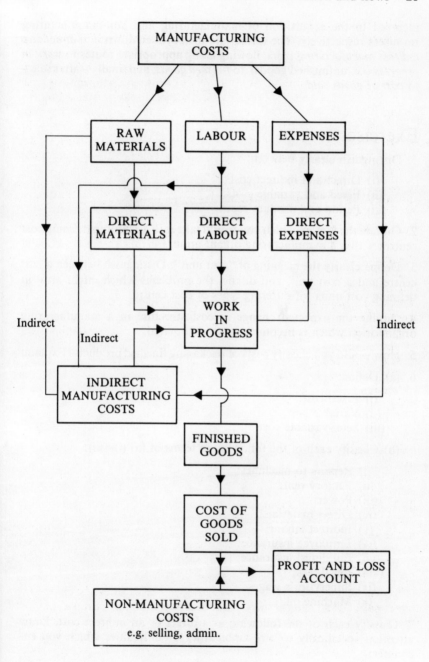

FIG. 6: **Flow of costs in a manufacturing organisation**

incurred in the acquisition of manufacturing and non-manufacturing resources respectively. The former are then broken down into *direct* and *indirect manufacturing costs*, flowing along appropriate routes to *work in progress* (i.e. unfinished goods), to *finished goods*, and finally – after sale – to *cost of goods sold*.

Exercises

1. Distinguish clearly between:

  (i) Direct and indirect costs;
  (ii) Fixed and variable costs;
  (iii) Period and product costs.

2. Outline the factors which you would take into account in defining cost centres within a manufacturing organisation.

3. Define clearly the meaning of "cost unit". Distinguish between a cost centre and a cost unit, and discuss the problems which might arise in defining cost units for differing types of cost centre.

4. Outline the expected change in cost structure in a manufacturing organisation which is becoming more automated.

5. How would you classify costs of packaging finished products? Explain.

6. (a) Define:

  (i) Fixed cost;
  (ii) Variable cost;
  (iii) Semi-variable cost.

  (b) Classify each of the following in terms of (a) (i)-(iii):

  (i) Repairs to machines;
  (ii) Factory rent;
  (iii) Power;
  (iv) Direct materials;
  (v) Indirect labour;
  (vi) Employee insurance;
  (vii) Buildings' insurance;
  (viii) Legal fees;
  (ix) Supervisor's wages;
  (x) Machine oil.

7. Classify each of the following as a direct or an indirect cost. Draw attention specifically to any ambiguities or difficulties which you encounter:

 (i) Salesmen's salaries;
 (ii) Vacation pay;
 (iii) Sick pay;
 (iv) Employee insurance;
 (v) Storeman's wages;
 (vi) Directors' fees;
 (vii) Managing director's salary;
(viii) Salary of quality control engineer;
 (ix) Salary of design engineer.

Chapter 3

Materials: purchasing, valuation and control

3.1 Purchasing

Although we are not concerned in this book with a detailed examination of administrative procedures and the accompanying documentation, a brief outline is necessary.

Purchase of materials is normally initiated by a stores manager, the person responsible for production control, or a departmental manager. The first of these would be interested in ensuring that supplies of standard input materials are available when needed, the second in ensuring the provision of any non-standard materials needed in production, and the third with individual departmental needs. In each case a *purchase requisition* would be sent to the *purchasing department*. A buyer in that department would then be responsible for finding a supplier of the required materials, and issuing to that supplier a *purchase order*.

Normally copies of the purchase order would be sent to the requisitioning department, to notify them that an order had been placed, and to the *goods inward department* (sometimes called the *goods received department*) to alert them to the impending arrival of the materials.

When the materials arrive at the goods inward department, a *goods-received note* is prepared detailing the date of receipt, the supplier, the quantity and quality of the materials received and so on. Copies of the goods-received note would normally be sent to the requisitioning person or department (with the materials), to the accounts department (for payment) and to the purchasing department. A copy would be retained in the goods-inward department. The procedure is summarised in Fig. 7, whilst in Fig. 8 (i)–(iii) are shown typical examples of the various documents involved.

Although the process is a simple one in principle, three key areas of responsibility can be identified. In the first place the person or persons raising the requisition order have a responsibility to do so in a timely manner in order that materials are available when needed. They must also, of course, act responsibly in requisitioning only materials which are necessary to the proper operation of the organisation. Secondly, the buyer

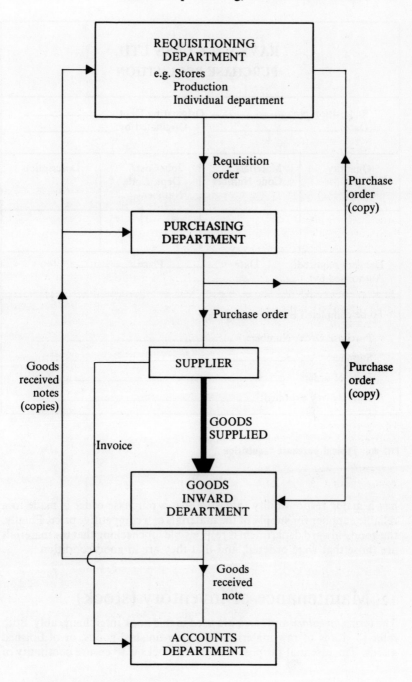

FIG. 7: Purchasing procedure

RAVEN & GLASS LTD.
PURCHASE REQUISITION

Requisition No:——————— Originating Dept:———————
Date:——————— Originated by:———————

Quantity	Materials Code Number	Job/Cost/ Dept. Code Number	Description

Delivery required: Date ——————— Place———————
Authorised by: ———————

To be completed by Purchasing Dept:

Purchase Order Number: ———————

Supplier: ———————

Date of order: ———————

Date delivey expected: ———————

FIG. 8(i): **Typical purchase requisition**

has a major responsibility to ensure that a purchase order is made to a reliable supplier for supply of the materials at a competitive price. Finally, the goods-inward department is responsible for checking that the materials are those that were ordered, and that they are in good condition.

3.2 Maintenance of inventory (stock)

The terms *inventory* and *stock* are used in this book interchangeably. Both refer to stores of raw materials, of partly-finished goods, or of finished goods. The essential purpose of holding stocks is to ensure continuity of

---

RAVEN & GLASS LTD.

PURCHASE ORDER

To: _____   Purchase Order No: _____
    _____   Date: _____
    _____   Requisition No: _____
    _____   Your ref: _____
    _____   Our ref: _____
                               Date delivery required: _____
                               Deliver to: _____

Quantity	Code Number	Description	Unit Price	Price

Please supply above in accordance with attached conditions:

Signed:_____ Per Raven & Glass Ltd.
        BUYER

FIG. 8(ii): **Typical purchase order**

manufacture in response to changing patterns of supply, demand, and productivity. If, for example, no stocks of raw materials were held then an increase in production to meet increased sales demand could be delayed whilst orders were placed with, and met by, an outside supplier. Furthermore, stocks will be helpful if shortages of raw materials occur.

From a practical point of view it is obviously necessary to keep records of movements in and out of inventory so that the inventory's contents are known at any time. Within a *stores ledger* is kept a separate *stock account* for each type of item held in stock. Corresponding to each account is a *stores ledger* (or *bin*) *card*, also sometimes called a stock control card.

RAVEN & GLASS LTD.

GOODS RECEIVED NOTE

G R N Number: _____   Supplier: _____
Date: _____
Purchase Order No: _____   Delivery date: _____

Quantity	Materials code number	Job/cost/ Dept. code number	Description

Goods received by: _____
Goods checked by: _____

FIG. 8(iii): **Typical goods received note**

These (held by the stores manager) differ from the stores ledger accounts (held by the accounts department) in that they exclude price information. When the stores manager receives materials for placing in stock, he is able from the accompanying copy of the goods-received note, to make a "receipts" entry on the appropriate stores ledger card. Those wishing to use items from stock must provide the stores-keeper with a *materials requisition order*. The stores keeper can then issue the required items from stock, making an "issues" entry on the appropriate stores ledger card which matches the details on the requisition order. A typical example of a stores ledger card is shown in Fig. 9. In the event that the requisitioned items proved to be in excess of requirements a *materials returned note* – very similar in format to the requisition order – can be used to record a transfer back into stores. Obviously a matching entry would be made to the appropriate stores ledger account.

The type of stock recording outlined above, allied with the recording of the balance of stock after each movement into or out of inventory, is known as the *perpetual inventory method*. In order to ensure its accurate

RAVEN & GLASS LTD.
STORES LEDGER CARD

Materials code No: _____   Minimum level: _____
Description: _____   Maximum level: _____
Card No: _____   Re-order level: _____
Location: _____   Re-order quantity: _____

Ref No	Date	Quantity received	Quantity issued	Balance

FIG. 9: **Typical stores ledger (bin) card**

operation, *stock-taking* is necessary once or more per year. This takes the form of a physical check of the contents of inventory. In a large organisation, holding stores perhaps of several hundred different types of items, small discrepancies between records and physical observation are not usually worth pursuing. It should be borne in mind, however, that some stock items may be very costly and others very inexpensive. Obviously, it is sensible to devote more time and attention to keeping accurate records of the former than of the latter. The keeping of accurate records on perhaps hundreds of stock items could be both laborious and very time-consuming if done manually. However, it is a routine operation, and therefore very suitable for computerisation. Increasingly, even small organisations are now relying on computerised stock-keeping records.

3.3 Inventory valuation

3.3.1 Introduction

An important feature of inventory policy relates to the costing of items issued to production from inventory. In times of stable prices this presents no problem. However, prices of raw materials, for example, are subject to change since they are purchased in markets outside the organisation, and therefore outside its control. Identical items in inventory may therefore have been acquired at very different prices. Short of attaching to each stock item a note of its purchase cost when it is received, it is difficult to know at what price materials issued from stores should be charged to production.

Several basic approaches can be used, and each is considered in turn using the following assumed schedule of purchases and issues for the month of October, which commences with an opening balance of 17 units @ £9/unit:

| Date | Purchases | | Issues | Balance |
	No. of units	£/unit	(No. of units)	(No. of units)
Oct 1	—	—	—	17
Oct 5	—	—	10	7
Oct 8	7	9.50	—	14
Oct 12	—	—	8	6
Oct 22	9	10.00	—	15
Oct 29	—	—	7	8
Oct 30	4	10.50	—	12
Oct 31	—	—	5	7

3.3.2 Last in first out (LIFO)

This policy charges issues from stores to production at the most recent purchase price. In other words, it assumes that those materials last received in inventory are the first to be issued from inventory to production. Using the schedule of §3.3.1 this would proceed as follows:

Date	Issue/Purchase	Balance	
		Composition	Total Value (£)
Oct 1	—	17 @ £9.00	153.00
Oct 5	Issue 10 @ £9.00	7 @ £9.00	63.00
Oct 8	Purchase 7 @ £9.50	7 @ £9.00 7 @ £9.50	129.50
Oct 12	Issue 7 @ £9.50 1 @ £9.00	6 @ £9.00	54.00
Oct 22	Purchase 9 @ £10.00	6 @ £9.00 9 @ £10.00	144.00
Oct 29	Issue 7 @ £10.00	6 @ £9.00 2 @ £10.00	74.00
Oct 30	Purchase 4 @ £10.50	6 @ £9.00 2 @ £10.00 4 @ £10.50	116.00
Oct 31	Issue 4 @ £10.50 1 @ £10.00	6 @ £9.00 1 @ £10.00	64.00

The major advantage of using this method is that relatively recent prices of raw materials are reflected in the charge to production. By the same token, however, since the general trend of prices is likely to be one of increase, it does mean that inventory remaining is progressively under-valued at increasingly out-of-date prices. A further implication is that the lower the figure placed on stock valuation, the lower is the net profit figure in the profit and loss account.

3.3.3 First in first out (FIFO)

This second method adopts the opposite approach by assuming that those items issued are charged at the oldest price. Naturally, the effect is to avoid the possibility – inherent under a LIFO system – of retaining stock at out-of-date prices: only the most recent prices are attached to inventory, and therefore remaining stock is valued at those prices. However, in a period of rapidly rising prices it does mean that charges to production may be unrealistically low. FIFO does have an advantage over LIFO in that it conforms more naturally to the physical flow of materials. After all, one would expect that those items held in stock for the longest time would be used first.

The FIFO system is applied to our previous example as follows:

Date	Issue/Purchase	Balance	
		Composition	Total Value (£)
Oct 1	—	17 @ £9.00	153.00
Oct 5	Issue 10 @ £9.00	7 @ £9.00	63.00
Oct 8	Purchase 7 @ £9.50	7 @ £9.00 7 @ £9.50	129.50
Oct 12	Issue 7 @ £9.00 1 @ £9.50	6 @ £9.50	57.00
Oct 22	Purchase 9 @ £10.00	6 @ £9.50 9 @ £10.00	147.00
Oct 29	Issue 6 @ £9.50 1 @ £10.00	8 @ £10.00	80.00
Oct 30	Purchase 4 @ £10.00	8 @ £10.00 4 @ £10.50	122.00
Oct 31	Issue 5 @ £10.00	3 @ £10.00 4 @ £10.50	72.00

During a time of rising prices FIFO, which values stock more highly than LIFO, will lead to a higher net income figure than will LIFO.

3.3.4 Weighted average (AVCO)

Although less of a problem with computerised records it will be appreciated from working through the last two examples that both LIFO and FIFO do involve considerable computational effort and detailed record keeping. Both, furthermore, can give rise to difficulties of comparison between similar jobs since costs to be charged to production depend very much on the order in which issues take place from stock.

No ideal solution exists. However, to use a *weighted average price* does avoid some of the problems inherent in both LIFO and FIFO. In the first place, detailed past records need not be kept, and calculations are reduced to a minimum. Secondly, two jobs simultaneously undertaken will have costs charged to them similarly, rather than in an arbitrary way depending on order of issue.

Again referring to our previous data this third approach is illustrated in detail:

Date	Issue/Purchase	Balance		
		Total value (£)	No. of units	Average price/unit (£)
Oct 1	—	153.00	17	9.00
Oct 5	Issue 10 @ £9.00	63.00	7	9.00
Oct 8	Purchase 7 @ £9.50	129.50	14	9.25
Oct 12	Issue 8 @ £9.25	55.50	6	9.25
Oct 22	Purchase 9 @ £10.00	145.50	15	9.70
Oct 29	Issue 7 @ £9.70	77.60	8	9.70
Oct 30	Purchase 4 @ £10.50	119.60	12	9.97
Oct 31	Issue 5 @ £9.97	69.77	7	9.97

3.3.5 Standard cost system

A final method of stock valuation involves the use of standard prices, see §§9.4, 9.5. Although this suffers from the normal difficulties surrounding forecasts, and from the investment in time needed to produce agreed standards, the advantages are considerable. In the first place, there is no variation in issue prices. In the second place, and perhaps more importantly, such an approach carries all the advantages of a standard costing system from the viewpoint of control. Thus deviations between actual and standard prices are readily revealed, and can be used to show inefficiencies (and efficiencies) in, for example, purchasing. Standard costing is examined in detail in Chapter 9.

Although a variety of other stock valuation systems exists those which have been described here are the most commonly used and the most important.

3.4 Inventory control

3.4.1 The problem

The key to determining an inventory control policy lies in analysing the costs involved in replenishing inventory and in holding units in inventory. On the one hand, associated with holding stocks there are costs of warehousing, obsolescence, invested capital, insurance, and deterioration. Additionally, for each order placed there will be associated clerical and administrative costs, which are likely to depend more upon the number of orders placed than upon their individual sizes. Clearly, a balance needs to be struck between the frequency and size of orders, and the need to have sufficient stocks on hand at any time in order to meet likely demands.

To keep the problem as simple as possible we make a number of assumptions concerning the cost structure. Firstly we suppose that the cost of placing an order, or _order cost_ involving invoicing and so on, is a fixed cost independent of the size of the order: we call it C_O. Thus, if in a particular period n orders are placed with the outside supplier the total ordering cost will be nC_O. Our second assumption is that the cost of holding one unit in inventory per unit time, or _holding cost_, is C_H. We are therefore supposing that the cost of holding a unit directly proportional

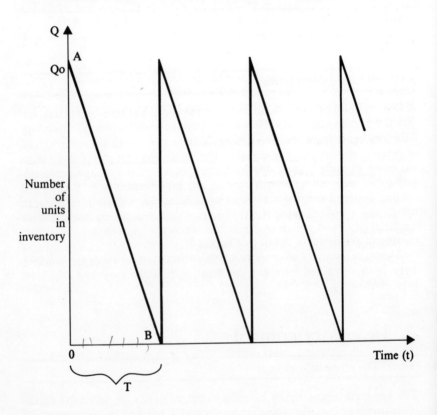

FIG. 10: **Basic inventory model**

to the length of time for which it is held, and that the total holding costs per unit time are directly proportional to the number of units held. Thus if Q (for quantity) units are held for time t then the total holding costs will be QTC_H. We now make two further assumptions about the demand for, and the supply of, the particular stock item:

(i) demand is constant;
(ii) replenishment is instantaneous.

The implications here are that the rate of issue from inventory to production is constant, and that placement of an order is followed immediately by supply into inventory. At this stage it is helpful to refer to Fig. 10, which presents graphically the implications of (i) and (ii) above.

We see that the inventory follows a cyclical pattern. At time $t = 0$ it is assumed that the inventory stands at a level of Q_O units. We see a steady fall in inventory level to zero after time T has elapsed. The gradient, D, of line AB, i.e.

$$\frac{Q_O}{T}$$

represents the constant rate of issue from inventory. At time T an order for Q_O further units is placed and immediately met. The process then continues through another identical cycle. The total costs, C_T, incurred in one cycle are:

$$C_T = \text{Ordering Costs} + \text{Holding Costs} \tag{1}$$

3.4.2 Economic order quantity (EOQ)

The mathematical argument which follows may be omitted by the reader. However, the result in equation (6), and its use in the worked example, are important.

We note that during one cycle the number of units held in stock ranges from Q_O (at time 0) to zero (at time T), with an average value of $\frac{Q_O}{2}$. The holding costs per cycle are therefore easily found as $\left(\frac{Q_O}{2}\right)C_HT$.

Thus:

$$C_T = C_O + \left(\frac{Q_O}{2}\right)C_HT \tag{2}$$

Since the cycle is T units of time long, the costs per unit time C_U, of the inventory policy, are:

$$C_U = \frac{C_T}{T} = \frac{C_O}{T} + \left(\frac{Q_O}{2}\right)C_H \tag{3}$$

We also know that demand D relates to Q_O and T as follows:

$$D = Q_O/T, \text{ or } T = Q_O/D \tag{4}$$

Thus we can write, from (3) and (4):

$$C_U = \frac{C_o}{Q_o/D} + \left(\frac{Q_o}{2}\right)C_H$$

$$= \left(\frac{DC_o}{Q_o}\right) + \left(\frac{Q_o}{2}\right)C_H \tag{5}$$

Presumably D, C_o, and C_H are relatively fixed in value. The only variable quantity which is under our control is Q_o, i.e. the quantity contained in each order. It is interesting to note that the first component (i.e. the ordering component) in equation 5 decreases as Q_o increases. This we would expect, since if we increase the size of our order we will reduce the number of orders which it is necessary to make. On the other hand, increasing Q_o means that the average level of our inventory will increase, and therefore our holding costs will increase. The situation is shown graphically in Fig. 11.

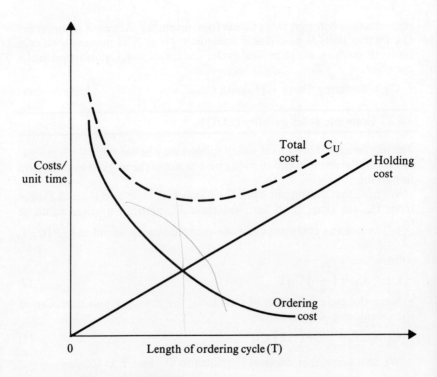

FIG. 11: **Inventory costs/unit time**

The full lines represent holding costs/unit time and ordering costs/unit time respectively, whilst the dotted line gives the sum of these. It can be seen that the minimum value of total cost/unit time occurs when holding costs/unit time and ordering costs/unit time are in fact equal*.

$$\text{i.e. when } \frac{DC_O}{Q_O} = \left(\frac{Q_O}{2}\right) C_H$$

$$\text{i.e. } Q_O = \sqrt{\left(\frac{2DC_O}{C_H}\right)} \tag{6}$$

Using this formula, we have a means now of calculating the optimal number of units to order each cycle in order to minimise total costs.

WORKED EXAMPLE

Suppose the cost of placing orders for a component is £100/order. Demand for the component is 2000/month. Warehousing and other holding costs are £2/unit/week.

The economic order quantity (EOQ) is calculated as follows:

$$EOQ = \sqrt{\frac{2 \times 2000 \times 100}{8}}$$

$$= 224 \text{ (to nearest integer).}$$

Note that consistent units must be used. Demand is given per month, and therefore holding costs/unit must be expressed as £8/month, rather than £2/week.

The formula (6) gives the value for Q_O which is known as the *economic order quantity* (EOQ). The mathematical model developed in this section is referred to as the *square-root inventory control model*.

3.4.3 Modifications to basic model

It was pointed out that a number of simplifying assumptions were made in deriving the EOQ model. Although these are unrealistic the model is not completely invalid. Inspection, for example, of the graph in Fig. 11 reveals that the total cost curve, C_U has a fairly shallow profile. This means that values of Q some way from the optimal EOQ value nevertheless give rise to values of C_U quite near the minimum.

However, it is not too difficult to remove the assumption of immediate

---

* Mathematically, C_U is a maximum or minimum when:

$$\frac{dC_U}{dQ_O} = -\frac{DC_O}{Q^2_O} + \frac{C_H}{2} = 0, \text{ i.e. } Q_O = \sqrt{\left(\frac{2DC_O}{C_H}\right)}$$

replenishment by assuming that once an order is placed units arrive in inventory at a constant rate over a period of time. The modified version of Fig. 10 then appears as in Fig. 12.

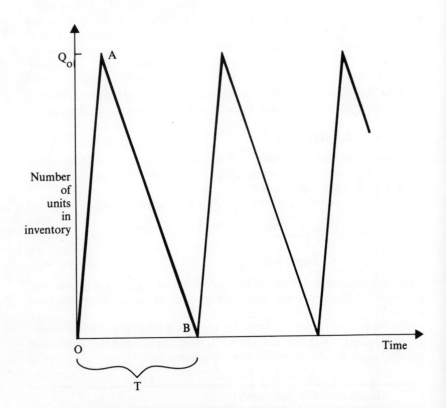

FIG. 12: **Basic inventory model modified for non-instantaneous replenishment**

Here, the gradient of AB does not represent the rate of arrival in inventory, but the net rate of arrival, i.e. the difference between the rate of supply and the rate of withdrawal, D. It can be shown that in these circumstances the modified version of equation 6 is:

$$Q_0' = \sqrt{\left\{ \frac{2DC_0}{(1 + \dfrac{D}{P}) C_H} \right\}} \qquad (7)$$

where p is the gradient of AB. Inspection of Equation 7 shows that when p is very large (i.e. when the rate of supply approaches instant) we recover Equation 6.

Alternatively, it may be that – although an order is met completely by one delivery into stock – there is some delay, known as the *lead time*, between placing an order and receiving it. In this case it would obviously be wise to place the order while some stocks still remain. Assuming still that demand, D, remains constant, if the lead time is L then the number of units to be issued between placing and receiving the order is LD. The appropriate time at which to order is when inventory stocks fall to level LD (see Fig. 13).

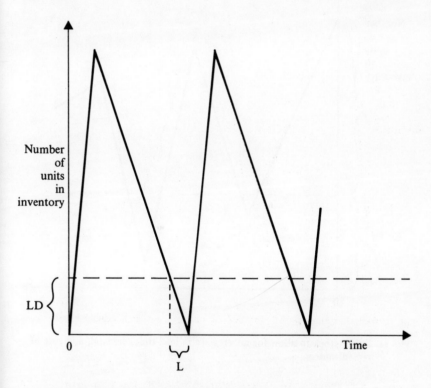

FIG. 13: **Lead-time between placing order and first receipts into inventory**

In practice, one of the major limitations of the model, however, is not that demand or supply rates may vary, but that it is assumed their patterns are known with certainty. In the real world, demand may change following changes in sales policy, machine breakdowns may affect productivity, and supplies of raw materials exactly in the required quantities at the right time and at the right price cannot be guaranteed.

A common policy is therefore to underpin the type of cycle assumed above by a *buffer-stock*. This system involves re-ordering when stocks fall to a pre-determined positive level, rather than to zero. This is shown graphically in Fig. 14.

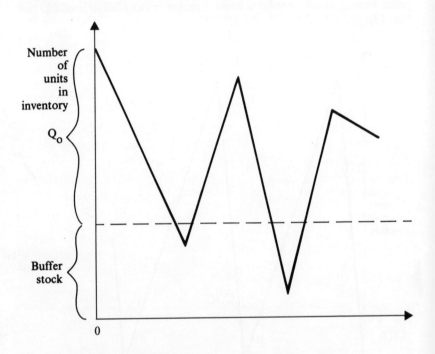

FIG. 14: **Buffer-stock to allow for uncertainty in lead-time, demand, and rate of replenishment.**

Exercises

1. Outline a method for recording materials receipt in a Goods Received department, explaining the nature and function of the documentation involved.

2. Consider the possible aims, within a manufacturing organisation, of a system of materials accounting.

3. Stock (inventory) planning and control is an important element of a management accounting system. What are its major features, and what are the practical difficulties which arise in its design and implementation?

4. Enumerate the various methods of pricing the issue of raw materials from stores, explaining the advantages and disadvantages of each.

5. Explain how you would identify over-investment in stocks, and how you would develop a policy to remove this.

6. Compare and contrast each of the following methods of pricing materials issue from stores:

  (i) FIFO;
  (ii) LIFO;
  (iii) Weighted average.

7. List the factors to be taken into account in calculating the economic order quantity. Illustrate the calculation of this quantity graphically and analytically.

8. To what extent is it necessary to have an annual stock valuation when using a perpetual inventory system? Discuss.

9. Describe in detail how you might operate a perpetual inventory system.

10. Design a stores ledger card for use in a manufacturing organisation having a wide range of differing stock items, and discuss the operation of the system to which it relates.

11. The following information concerns stocks of component A during the month of October. There was no opening stock on 1 October.

Receipts   2 Oct   8 tonnes @ £20 per tonne
            5 Oct   5 tonnes @ £22 per tonne
         19 Oct 6 tonnes @ £23 per tonne
         29 Oct 2 tonnes @ £24 per tonne

Issues   3 Oct   4 tonnes
            8 Oct   5 tonnes
         20 Oct 7 tonnes
         30 Oct 3 tonnes

Find:

  (i) the issue values under a FIFO system;
  (ii) the issue values under a LIFO system;

(iii) the weighted average price after each issue of stock taking.

12. The prices of many raw materials are liable to fluctuate with changing political, social, and economic factors. Periods of stability may be followed by periods of increasing or decreasing prices.

Discuss in the context of a particular material with which you are familiar the factors likely to affect its price, and explain your choice of a valuation policy for issues of this material from stock.

13. The following information relates to stocks of item X during June:

Opening inventory		90kg @ £4.25/kg
Purchases:	2 June	75kg @ £4.00/kg
	3 June	100kg @ £4.25/kg
	7 June	200kg @ £4.50/kg
	12 June	100kg @ £4.20/kg
	25 June	50kg @ £4.60/kg
	28 June	200kg @ £4.30/kg
Issues:	6 June	150kg
	12 June	200kg
	18 June	175kg
	29 June	160kg

Compute the issues of item X during June on a:

(i) LIFO basis;
(ii) FIFO basis.

Chapter 4

Labour: costing and control

4.1 Payment schemes

There are two major principles upon which payments to employees are based. The first relates payment to the measured output achieved by the employee, and gives rise to *piecework schemes*. Under such a scheme an employee processing 200 units of product, would receive 10 times the payment of an employee processing 20 units. Piecework schemes suffer from a number of disadvantages, and tend to be of limited application in a manufacturing context. A worker may, under such a scheme, be penalised through no fault of his own. For example, low productivity earlier in the manufacturing process, shortage of essential raw materials, or machine breakdowns may all cause his productivity to be low. A problem for the employer is that piecework schemes encourage employees to work as quickly as possible in order to increase their output, with the result that the quality of finished products may be poor. Furthermore, employees may be tempted to ignore safety regulations in their keenness to maximise output.

The second principle relates payments to the time for which an employee works. *Time-related schemes*, based upon agreed hourly wage rates, are very common, although they too have disadvantages. Most importantly a pure scheme of this type provides no incentive to the employee to achieve either high quality or quantity of output. Employees producing 20 units and 200 units would receive equal payments. An employee knows that if he works for the agreed number of hours per day he will be paid at the agreed rate per hour. It might be useful at this point to distinguish between the salaried employee and the wage earner. Both are paid on a time-related basis. However, the salary earner would normally receive an agreed annual salary, paid monthly in twelve equal payments. The wage earner would normally receive each week a payment calculated by multiplying the number of hours worked in that week by the agreed hourly wage rate.

In practice, payment schemes are often based upon a compromise between the two principles of piecework and time-related earnings. Such a compromise needs to recognise that an employee needs some security of income, but also an incentive to work efficiently and effectively.

4.2 Bonus schemes

4.2.1 Premium bonus schemes

Under a standard costing system predetermined standards exist for the times associated with particular processes on product units. (These are considered in more detail in Chapter 9. They are theoretical times based upon what an employee should achieve under certain specified conditions. Practical achievement is compared with the theoretical standard.) In principle it is a simple matter to design a system of bonus payments to an employee who completes a task in less than the standard time. Such a bonus system typically rewards the employee in terms of part of the cost which he has saved:

WORKED EXAMPLE

$$\text{Bonus payment (B)} = \left(\begin{array}{l}\text{Standard time (S) for task}\\ - \text{Actual time (A) for task}\end{array}\right)$$

$$\times \text{Hourly rate (R)}$$

$$\times \text{Agreed proportion (P)}$$

i.e. $B = (S - A) RP$

Suppose:

Standard time	(S)	=	5 hours
Actual time	(A)	=	$3\frac{1}{2}$ hours
Hourly rate	(R)	=	£4

Then, B   = £$(5 - 3\frac{1}{2})$ 4P
                   = £6P

A system such as this, using a percentage allocation of the "cost of time saved" between employer and employee, is known as a *Halsey type system*. The value of proportion P, lying between 0% and 100%, is fixed by prior agreement between employer and employees. With P = 60% the employee's bonus payment would be £3.60, and the total payment due to the employee would be:

(AR + B)

i.e. £$(3\frac{1}{2} \times 4 + 3.60)$ = £17.60.

The *Rowan system* is a modified version of this approach. It uses a variable, rather than a fixed, value for the proportion P. Specifically,

$$P = \frac{\text{actual time for task}}{\text{standard time for task}} \quad \frac{(A)}{(S)}$$

Thus, $\qquad B = (S - A) R \dfrac{A}{S}$

and,
Total payment

$$= AR + (S - A) \frac{AR}{S}$$

$$= AR \left(2 - \frac{A}{S}\right)$$

$$= £3\frac{1}{2} \times 4 \times \left(2 - \frac{3\frac{1}{2}}{5}\right)$$

$$= £18.20$$

The bonus payments due under the two schemes are compared in Fig. 15 for varying values of the ratio A/S. We note that the maximum bonus payment under the Rowan system occurs when the actual time, A, for the task is just half the standard time, S. The bonus due under Halsey is greater (less) than that due under Rowan if A/S is less (greater) than P. In Fig. 16 we illustrate the rates of payment (including bonus) under the two

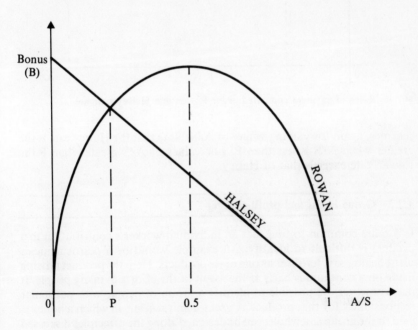

FIG. 15: **Comparison of bonus payments under Halsey and Rowan systems**

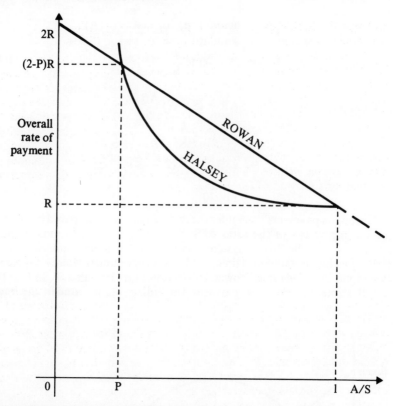

FIG. 16: **Rates of payment compared under Rowan and Halsey schemes**

schemes, again for varying values of A/S. Note that the Halsey rate is the greater when A/S is less than P. For values of A/S greater than P the Rowan rate exceeds that of Halsey.

4.2.2 Group bonus and profit-sharing

It is quite common to find that an individual worker's contribution to a product is difficult to identify. An example would be a petrochemicals plant having say, fertiliser as one of its products. Here the product is being made on a continuous basis as the result of the efforts of many people. It may, however, be possible to identify a group of people with particular responsibility for that product. A *group bonus scheme*, in which a bonus is paid to the group as a whole, can be designed along the principles discussed in §4.2.1. Obviously, the method of distribution of any bonus payment amongst the individual workers in the group needs to be agreed by all concerned in advance.

Although no bonus system is without disadvantage a scheme which has become increasingly popular in recent years is based upon *profit-sharing*. Here, the workforce may be rewarded at the end of the financial year if profits exceed those targeted. Unfortunately, this can soon become expected practice and in hard times the absence of a bonus can lead to considerable dissatisfaction. As a variant of this, workers may be granted shares in the company, rather than cash. This has the advantage that part ownership of the company will provide the employees with a continuing interest in the welfare of the company, and a continuing motivation towards efficiency and high productivity.

4.3 Labour-related costs

Although wages and salaries form the major part of labour costs, there are a number of other related costs which need to be recognised.

For hours worked in excess of an agreed norm, or at difficult times (perhaps evenings or weekends) it is customary to pay employees at a different rate. This *overtime rate* might typically be $1\frac{1}{2}$ times the normal hourly wage rate. In accounting for overtime costs it is necessary to separate the *overtime premium* (i.e. the excess in hourly rate) from the normal rate. Treatment of this overtime premium varies. If, for example, overtime work has been necessary because of a shortage of labour or because of a general increase in demand for the company's products, the overtime premium may be classified as an indirect labour cost, and therefore part of indirect manufacturing costs. On the other hand, if a contract for a specific job is falling behind schedule and overtime work is necessary to meet a customer's deadline, it would be appropriate to classify the overtime premium as a direct labour cost of that contract.

Even in the most efficient operation delays in production occur. These may be due to machine breakdowns, to temporary shortages of raw materials, to inefficiencies elsewhere, or to transfer of operatives between different tasks. Some *idle-time* is inevitable, and must be accepted as normal. However, the cost of idle-time needs to be accounted for separately from direct labour costs. If this is not done, abnormally high idle-time will go undetected, and no remedial action will be taken. Usually the cost of idle-time will be treated as an indirect manufacturing cost.

Some of the more significant remaining labour-related costs are holiday pay, sick pay, advertising and other recruitment costs, training, employer's insurance payments, employer's contributions to pension funds, and provision of employees' welfare facilities. All of these are normally charged as indirect labour costs to the appropriate overhead account.

RAVEN & GLASS LTD.
TIME SHEET

Employee name: _____ Week No: _____
Employee number: _____

Date	Start time	Finish time	Task details	Office use		
				Hours worked	Rate of pay	Pay
					Total Pay	

Signed: _____
Supervisor

FIG. 17: **Typical time-sheet**

4.4 Recording of labour costs

The detailed recording and analysing of labour costs is a complex affair. We shall be concerned here with the principles involved.

Since most payment systems are basically time-related the recording of numbers of hours worked is obviously of vital importance. Normally, each hourly-paid worker has his own individual *time-* or *clock-card*. On his arrival at work the card is inserted into a time clock which punches the time of arrival on to the card. Similarly, when he leaves work the card is punched with his departure time. The time-card, which is usually replaced at the beginning of each week, therefore maintains a record of the number of hours spent at work by each employee.

Although the clock-card contains the bare information necessary to calculate the employee's earnings, it does not give the detailed information necessary for labour cost analysis. This information is collected on a *time-sheet*. On this are entered the times an employee began and finished working on a particular job. At the end of the day, or week, the time-sheets and clock-cards should be reconciled in order to check on each employee's activities. The time-sheets also, of course, provide the information necessary for charging labour costs to cost centres or cost units. A typical time-sheet is shown in Fig. 17. The flow of labour costs information is illustrated in Fig. 18.

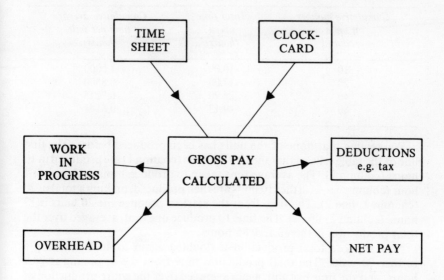

FIG. 18: **Flow of labour costs information**

4.5 Learning curves

In a manufacturing organisation many of the operations performed by the workers are repetitive. On a motor-car production line, for example, an individual may be responsible for assembling particular components, or painting particular areas of the vehicle's body. Observation has shown that repetitive tasks are subject to a *learning effect*. Indeed, in everyday life we know that the more often we repeat a task, such as attaching an electrical plug to an appliance, the shorter the time needed to complete the task. The learning effect can be analysed quantitatively, and it is important to do so when estimating future labour costs. Although strictly falling within the realm of budgeting (see Chapter 8), the effect is discussed here since it is specifically related to labour.

It has been found that the decrease in time necessary to complete a task follows a specific pattern. The *average-time learning curve* is based upon the assumption that when the cumulative number of units produced doubles, then the cumulative average time to produce a unit decreases by a constant percentage. This percentage is usually found to lie between 5% and 30%. Consider the following illustrative data:

Cumulative number of units produced	Total time taken (hours)	Cumulative average time per unit (hours)
10	10.00	1.0000
20	17.00	0.8500
40	28.90	0.7225
80	49.13	0.6141

We assume that none of the units has been produced before. The first line of the table tells us that the first 10 units (column 1) are produced in 10 hours (column 2). The average time taken to produce 1 unit is therefore 1 hour (column 3). A further 10 units are then produced, making a total of 20 (column 1, line 2). The time from the start to produce the 20 units is 17 hours (column 2, line 2). The time to produce one unit, averaged over the total production is therefore 0.85 hours.

Now suppose total production is doubled again to 40 by making a further 20 units. The total production time from the beginning is 28.9 hours, and the time per unit, again averaged over the entire production of 40, is 0.7225 hours. The final row in the table is derived from a further doubling of total production to 80. The key relationship which captures the learning effect is contained in columns 1 and 3. Successive doublings of total production are seen to result in reductions of the cumulative average production time per unit by a factor of 85%:

i.e. $1 \times 0.85 = 0.85$;
$\quad 0.85 \times 0.85 = 0.7225$;
$\quad 0.2775 \times 0.85 = 0.6141$;
$\quad$ and so on.

The learning curve describing this behaviour is known as an *85% learning curve*. The curve is illustrated in Fig. 19. From this curve it is a simple matter to estimate the number of hours needed to produce inter-mediate numbers of total units.

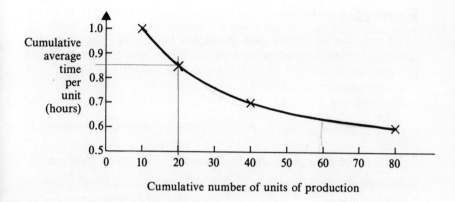

FIG. 19: **85% learning curve**

For example, if the total number of units to be produced were 67, the average time per unit would be 0.65 hrs., and the total time of manufacture 67 × 0.65 hrs. = 43.30 hrs.

Similarly, if a new order – say for 15 units – had been received after total production had reached 40, the labour hours required to produce the additional units can be readily calculated:

Total time for 55 units = 0.68 × 55 = 37.20 hrs.
Total time for 40 units = 0.72 × 40 = 28.90 hrs.

∴ Time for incremental 15 units is 8.30 hrs.

4.6 Use of learning curves

Usually labour costs are of more interest than labour hours. If the wage rate per hour is known, the direct labour cost can be calculated by multiplying that rate by the number of labour hours found from the learning curve. Furthermore, any costs which are closely related to direct labour costs can then be estimated. These might include, for example, some indirect manufacturing costs.

Obviously the learning curve has an important part to play in the budgeting of labour and labour-related costs. It also has a role in the setting of labour performance standards, since actual productivity can be compared with the learning curve predictions. Finally, learning curves can be used in the prediction of future labour requirements, given planned production levels.

Exercises

1. Discuss the objectives and principles underlying wage incentive schemes. Outline any advantages and disadvantages to such a scheme from the viewpoint of:

(i) Employer;
(ii) Employee.

2. Outline several different possible bases for incentive payments to employees.

3. Discuss the advantages and disadvantages of group bonus schemes.

4. How might the following be dealt with from an accounting viewpoint:

(i) Idle time;
(ii) Overtime premium.

5. Explain, with examples, the following:

(i) Halsey bonus scheme;
(ii) Rowan premium bonus scheme.

6. Distinguish clearly between indirect labour and direct labour. Classify the following as direct or indirect labour costs, justifying your choice:

(i) Vacation pay;
(ii) Salary of supervisor of a single cost centre;
(iii) Salary of supervisor of three different cost centres;
(iv) Wages of factory cleaner.

7. A number of costs are implicit in a high labour turnover rate, and are in addition to those arising from training and recruitment.

Consider these other costs which need to be recognised by the management, and how they might be controlled.

8. Explain why many manufacturing organisations choose to exclude overtime premium payments from the cost of manufacturing. What is your opinion with regard to the treatment of overtime payment in product costs?

9. Two salesmen, A and B, are employed by a wholesaler of foodstuffs. Data relating to their sales are as follows:

	A	B
Gross sales	£12,350	£7,100
Sales returns	£850	£100
Cost of goods sold	£9,000	£4,250
Expenses reimbursed	£275	£105
Other direct costs	£200	£23
Rate of commission on gross sales	6%	6%

Is there any indication that the policy of commission payments is not operating to the company's advantage?

10. The Pigeon Co. has in mind the introduction of an incentives scheme for its employees. Three possibilities are under consideration:

(i) Rowan:

Standard time/unit	12 mins
Wage rate/hour	£4
Hours worked	8
Actual production	49

(ii) Halsey:

Standard time/unit	12 mins
Wage rate/hour	£4
Hours worked	8
Actual production	47

(iii) Piece rate:

Standard time/unit	12 mins
Wage rate/hour	£4
Hours worked	8
Actual production	44

Compute under each system the wages payable per day, and the cost per unit:

(a) using the above data
(b) assuming a production increase of 4 units in each of (i) – (iii).

Assume under the Halsey scheme a previously agreed proportion rate, P, of 0.66.

Chapter 5

Overheads: classification, apportionment, and allocation

5.1 Introduction

In Chapter 2 several bases were introduced for the classification and analysis of costs. There we talked of *functional classification*:

  (i) *production* (or *manufacturing*)
 (ii) *selling*
(iii) *administration*
(iv) *research and development*

of cost elements:

  (i) *materials*
 (ii) *labour*
(iii) *expenses*

of:

  (i) *period costs* and
 (ii) *product costs*

and of:

  (i) *direct costs* and
 (ii) *indirect costs*

A major objective of cost analysis is to channel costs to, or identify costs with, products in order to provide information for pricing decisions. At this stage it is useful to review our progress towards achieving this. Firstly, in terms of the functional classifications it is very often the case that selling, administration and research and development costs are not distributed across product units. To do so is usually too difficult, unnatural, and time-consuming. There seems, for example, little meaning in attempting to break down the general costs of the typing pool and charge them to individual product units. Instead, all three of these functional classifications are treated not only as indirect costs, but as indirect period costs, i.e. they are charged against gross profit in the period in which they are incurred. This leaves us then with production, or manufacturing costs. Since these are firmly related to the production process it is natural to attempt to distribute such costs to products. By definition, the direct costs (of materials, labour, and expenses) present no problem. Remaining, however, we have the indirect costs (again of materials, labour, and expenses). The treatment of these *indirect manufacturing costs,* (or *manufacturing overhead, factory overhead*) forms the subject of this chapter.

A word of warning, however. No definitive "right" or "wrong" system exists for treating costs. Circumstances of a particular organisation, and the judgement of the management accountant, may favour charging some of selling costs or all research and development costs to production. We adopt the following treatment because it is relatively simple, relatively common, and because it can be adapted in a natural way to treat the other functional areas of cost where appropriate.

5.2 Apportionment, allocation, and absorption of overhead

At the outset it is helpful to distinguish between two stages in the treatment of overhead. To do so we recall our discussion of cost centres and cost units in Chapter 2.

The process of *cost allocation* is that whereby an entire cost item is charged to a cost centre or cost unit. For example, in a furniture factory glues could be sensibly classified as indirect materials. The assembly department would be a natural cost centre, and the one to which the entire cost of glues could be allocated (assuming glues to be used by the assembly department only). Similarly, on a motor-car production line we would allocate the cost of an engine to each vehicle as a cost unit.

However, it is often the case that a particular cost cannot be identified exclusively with one cost centre or one cost unit. For example, the benefits of lighting are shared by the whole factory, and therefore several cost centres. The costs of factory lighting cannot therefore be allocated (i.e. charged to a single cost centre or unit). Instead, these costs need to be distributed across a number of cost centres. The process of doing so is known as *cost apportionment*.

In analysing overhead, our first task is one of apportionment and allocation to cost centres, followed by allocation from cost centres to cost units. The actual numerical process, using application rates (see §5.5), of allocating overhead costs from cost centres to cost units is called *overhead absorption*.

5.3 Apportionment between production cost centres

It is important at this stage to underline the distinction between *production cost centres* and *service cost centres*. The former are those directly involved in the manufacturing process and might include, for example, machining, assembly, and finishing. Service departments, on the other hand, are not directly involved in the manufacturing process, although they are essential in maintaining the production process. They include power, personnel, machine maintenance, and so on. Their costs need to be apportioned to the producing departments in an objective way if we are to achieve our aim of eventually attaching all production-related costs to cost units.

The usual equitable approach is to apportion costs to cost centres on the basis of the benefit received by that cost centre. Although such an approach sounds sensible, difficulties arise in agreeing what benefits are received. For example, total power costs might be charged to cost centres in proportion to the usage of power in each of those cost centres. However, power costs are often levied on the basis of a fixed component – irrespective of usage – plus a variable component dependent on the number of kilowatt hours. Clearly, the variable component could be distributed to cost centres according to the metered usage in each. How should we apportion the fixed component, however?

Some examples follow. It should be noted, however, that bases of apportionment may vary according to the nature of the cost, and to the particular circumstances in the organisation:

Service cost	Basis of apportionment to production cost centre
Computing	Number of hours of machine time
Catering; employee welfare; employee insurance	Direct labour costs
Rent; rates; estates and buildings insurance	Floor area; department volume
Machine maintenance	Labour hours; labour cost; machine hours
Power	Metered usage; numbers of machine hours
Lighting	Floor area; number of lights

The following example illustrates the *direct method* for apportioning service centres' costs to producing centres. The calculations are self-explanatory:

| | Producing departments | | |
	Machining	Finishing	Total
Area (m²)	3,000	2,400	5,400
Direct labour costs (£)	24,000	96,000	120,000
Machine usage (hours)	1,800	450	2,250

| | Service departments | | |
	Power	Estates and buildings	Employee welfare
Costs to be allocated (£)	12,000	21,000	30,000
Basis of allocation	Machine usage (hours)	Area (m²)	Direct labour costs (£)

| | Direct apportionment of service departments' costs to producing departments (£) | | |
	Machining	Finishing	Total (£)
Power	9,600	2,400	12,000
Estates and buildings	11,667	9,333	21,000
Employee welfare	6,000	24,000	30,000

However, it should be borne in mind that apportionments are mechanical only once the basis has been decided. There may well be several possible other bases which could be used. Which is to be used is a matter for the experience and judgement of the accountant, and for agreement with and between those with responsibilities in relation to the production cost centres.

5.4 Cost apportionment between service cost centres

5.4.1 The problem

A complicating feature is that some of the overhead costs should properly
be charged from one service cost centre to another, before being charged
from a service cost centre to a production cost centre. For example, both
Power, and Salaries and wages are service cost centres. However, the Power
cost centre will employ people and Salaries and wages will use power for
heating, lighting, and the operation of business machines. Thus the
Salaries and wages cost centre should be apportioned some of the power
costs, and the Power cost centre should be apportioned some of the costs of
running the Salaries and wages department. There are two common
procedures for dealing with this type of situation.

5.4.2 Stepwise apportionment

In some cases the benefits provided by one service centre to another may be
insignificant. The input by Machine maintenance to Salaries and wages,
for example, is likely to fall into this category. The input provided by
Computing to Salaries and wages may, on the other hand, be quite large.
This suggests a practical procedure involving, firstly, selecting that
centre which services the greatest number of other centres. The costs of this
centre are then apportioned to the production centres and other service
centres. The remaining service centre providing the most service to others
is then selected, and its costs apportioned. The process continues until all
service centre costs have been apportioned to production centres. The
following example illustrates the procedure. Note that additional information concerning the areas, direct labour costs, and machine usages of
the three service departments themselves is needed:

	Producing departments		Service departments			
	Machin-ing	Finish-ing	Power	Estates and buildings	Employee welfare	Total
Area (m²)	3,000	2,400	50	—	90	5,540
Direct labour costs (£)	24,000	36,000	1,000	4,500	—	65,500
Machine usage (hours)	1,800	450	—	30	10	2,290

	Step-wise apportionment of service department costs to producing departments				
	Cost to allocate (£)	Power	Estates and buildings	Machining	Finishing
Employee welfare*	30,000	458	2,061	10,992	16,489
Estates and buildings	23,061	212	—	12,694	10,155
Power	12,670 (i.e. 12,000 +458 +212)	—	—	10,136	2,534
			Total	33,822	29,178

* Note that at each step a further component of the base is excluded from the calculation. Not to do so would result in charging of costs back to a department from which all costs had been charged out.

5.4.3 Reciprocal apportionment of service costs

In the above illustration, the service provided by Employee welfare to Estates and buildings is reflected in an apportionment to Estates and buildings of £2,061 of the costs of Employee welfare. However, any service provided by Estates and buildings to Employee welfare is ignored. Reciprocal apportionment recognises the approximate nature of the step-wise process, by casting the interrelationships as a set of linear equations. These are solved to find the exact apportionments. Using the same data as before:

	Producing Departments		Service Departments			Total
	Machin- ing	Finish- ing	Power	Estates and buildings	Employee welfare	
Area (m²)	3,000 (0.5415)	2,400 (0.4332)	50 (0.0090)	—	90 (0.0163)	5,540 (1.000)
Direct labour costs (£)	24,000 (0.3664)	36,000 (0.5496)	1,000 (0.0153)	4,500 (0.0687)	—	65,000 (1.000)
Machine usage (hours)	1,800 (0.7860)	450 (0.1965)	—	30 (0.0131)	10 (0.0044)	2,290 (1.000)

where the figures in brackets give the fractional parts of the allocation bases:

Suppose we set:

E = Estates and buildings
W = Employee welfare
P = Power

where each represents total service department costs after all reciprocal allocations between service departments have been completed. Each total cost is made up of the original departmental cost, augmented by allocations from each of the other service departments.

Thus:

$$E = 21{,}000 + 0.0687W + 0.0131P \qquad\qquad\text{(i)}$$
$$W = 30{,}000 + 0.0163E + 0.0044P \qquad\qquad\text{(ii)}$$
$$P = 12{,}000 + 0.0090E + 0.0153W* \qquad\qquad\text{(iii)}$$

Solving these three simultaneous equations gives:

E = £23,256.92
P = £12,674.96
W = £30,434.86

The final allocations therefore are:

*Manually these may be solved by firstly substituting for P from equation (iii) into equations (i) and (ii):

$$E = 21000 + 0.0687W + 0.0131 (12000 + 0.0090E + 0.0153W) \qquad\qquad\text{(iv)}$$
and
$$W = 30000 + 0.0163E + 0.0044 (12000 + 0.0090E + 0.0153W) \qquad\qquad\text{(v)}$$

Collecting terms together and simplifying:

$$0.9998821E = 21157.2 + 0.0689004W$$
$$0.9999327W = 300052.8 + 0.01633986E$$

i.e.
$$E = 21159.694 + 0.0689085W \qquad\qquad\text{(vi)}$$
and $$W = 30054.822 + 0.0163406E \qquad\qquad\text{(vii)}$$

Substituting now for W from (vii) into (vi) now gives:

$$E = 21159.694 + 0.0689085 (30054.822 + 0.0163406E)$$

Again simplifying by collecting terms we obtain

$$E = 23256.92$$

Finally W can now be found from (vii), and then P from any of (i), (ii), or (iii).

This process is very tedious. Readers familiar with simple matrix algebra will be able to solve (i)-(iii) more simply. Alternatively simple "computer packages" (i.e. pre-prepared programmes) are readily available for most micro-computers to relieve the calculations involved.

	Machining (£)	Finishing (£)
Estates and buildings	12,594 (0.5415)	10,075 (0.4332)
Employee welfare	11,151 (0.3664)	16,727 (0.5496)
Power	9,963 (0.7860)	2,491 (0.1965)
Total	33,708	29,293

5.5 Overhead absorption

Let us assume that the process of apportioning and allocating overhead costs to production cost centres is complete. The next stage in the process is that of allocating overhead costs to cost units, and for simplicity we shall assume that a cost unit is a single, discrete, unit of product. We need firstly, however, to draw a distinction between *fixed overhead* and *variable overhead*. It may come as a surprise to learn that variable overhead costs exist at all, since by definition overhead costs cannot be naturally associated with a cost unit, and yet variable costs are those varying with production level. Consider, however, machine maintenance costs. These cannot naturally be attached to a cost unit of product in the obvious way that direct materials and direct labour costs can. Nevertheless, following an increase in output of 50% one would expect maintenance costs to increase approximately proportionately: either because more machines were being used, or because existing machines were being put to increased use. On the other hand, insurance costs of the factory building will not depend upon production levels. In practice it can sometimes be difficult to distinguish between fixed overhead and variable overhead, and it is often the case that an overhead cost contains a component of each.

There are two subsequent alternative treatments of fixed and variable overhead: *absorption costing* and *marginal* (or *direct*) *costing* (see Chapter 6) respectively. The difference between the two is that in the former all overhead (i.e. fixed and variable) is *absorbed* (i.e. charged) to cost units. In the latter, only variable overhead is charged to cost units. The difference is an important one, and has far-reaching implications for the measurement of income and the valuation of stock, as we shall see in Chapter 6.

For the moment we shall assume a traditional absorption costing system. We shall therefore be concerned with both fixed and variable overhead, and their absorption to cost units (i.e. for the moment, units of product). Essentially, the problem is one of distributing the total overhead costs charged to a cost centre in a rational manner so that eventually they are charged to cost units. If product units passing through a cost centre were all exactly the same there would be no problem, since the total overhead would simply be divided by the number of product units, and the resulting figure charged to each unit. Unfortunately, such a simple situation rarely exists in practice. Instead, cost centres usually have a range of different product units associated with them, and single *overhead application rates* would not be sensible. Furthermore, different rates may need to be used for variable overhead and for fixed overhead. As a simple illustration, suppose that two products, A and B, pass through the machining department, and that twice the time is needed to machine a unit of A than is needed for a unit of B. It would not seem equitable to absorb the allocation of machine maintenance costs equally on each unit of A and B.

Two categories of base for devising *absorption* (or *application*) *rates* are normally available. The first is related to direct costs, and known as *on-cost rates*, whilst the second is related to time and called *hourly recovery rates*.

5.6 On-cost overhead application rates

Absorption (or application) rates can be calculated by dividing the overhead of the cost centre to be allocated by a chosen direct cost. Three types of direct cost may be used to develop the following application rates:

(i) *direct materials percentage rate*;
(ii) *direct labour percentage rate*;
(iii) *prime cost* (i.e. direct materials + direct labour) *percentage rate*.

The resulting rate in each case can then be used to absorb overhead to cost units as illustrated in the following example concerning Department X:

Direct Materials:	£5,000
Direct labour:	£2,500
Manufacturing overhead:	£4,000
Direct labour hours:	500
Machine hours	300

Thus (i) direct materials percentage rate: 80% (i.e. $\frac{4,000}{5,000} \times 100\%$)

(ii) direct labour percentage rate: 160% (i.e. $\frac{4,000}{2,500} \times 100\%$)

(iii) prime cost percentage rate: $53\frac{1}{3}\%$ (i.e. $\frac{4,000}{7,500} \times 100\%$)

Suppose now that the following information relates to a completed job, No. 27, passing through Department X:

Direct materials:	£250
Direct labour:	£180
Direct labour hours:	40
Machine hours:	20

The manufacturing overhead to be absorbed under the three different application rates by this job would be respectively:

$$\text{(i)} \quad £250 \times 80\% = £200$$
$$\text{or (ii)} \quad £180 \times 160\% = £288$$
$$\text{or (iii)} \quad £430 \times 53\% = £229$$

5.7 Hourly recovery overhead application rates

In a very similar way absorption rates can be derived by dividing the overhead to be absorbed by a measure of time. We obtain the following:

(i) *machine hour rate*;
(ii) *direct labour hours rate*.

Referring to the previous example:

(i) Machine hour rate: £13.33/hour
(ii) Direct labour hours rate: £8/hour

the manufacturing overhead to be absorbed by job 27 under the two approaches is

$$\text{(i)} \quad £20 \times 13.33 = £266.6$$
$$\text{or: (ii)} \quad £8 \times 40 = £320.$$

5.8 Comparison of absorption rates

Using different bases leads to different rates of allocation of overhead, as we have seen in §§5.6, and 5.7. The common feature is that all should result in the absorption of all the overhead to be applied. The most appropriate base to use in particular circumstances is a matter for the management accountant's individual judgement and experience. However, it is useful here to look at some of the more obvious considerations which need to be taken into account.

One objective might be to match the overhead costs with benefits received. A base needs to be used which is not only theoretically sound but which can also be applied simply and practically. A further important consideration in the choice is the factor which appears to bear the closest causal relationship to the overhead costs. In practice, a range of rates is likely to be used, varying across cost-centres, product types, producing departments, and origins of overhead (i.e. indirect labour, indirect materials, or indirect expenses).

Overhead costs are often time-related, and hourly recovery rates in theory more appropriate than on-cost rates. For example, in a highly mechanical production process using little direct labur the machine hour rate would be an obvious choice. A direct labour hours rate would be suitable when direct labour was predominant, and machine useage relatively small. Unfortunately, the additional administrative costs of collecting and analysing figures for total machine hours or total direct labour hours can be considerable.

Of the on-cost rates, direct labour cost percentage is probably the most popular and the most convenient. Care needs to be taken, however, if hourly rates of basic and overtime payments differ between employees and between jobs. The use of direct material cost as a base is relatively rare, since changes in the price of raw materials due to external factors are unlikely to affect the incidence of overhead. Such bases may be appropriate, however, in specialised industries using high-cost raw materials such as in the manufacture of pharmaceuticals and special alloys. Finally, prime cost is fairly simple to use, and does acknowledge the fact that both direct materials and direct labour costs have a relation to overhead. By the same token, however, a prime cost percentage rate suffers the disadvantages of both direct labour and direct materials bases.

5.9 Pre-determined overhead rates

In §§5.6 and 5.7 figures of, for example, direct labour hours, direct labour costs, total overhead, were all given. Calculation of the rate was simple. Unfortunately in practice none of these figures will be known until the end of the accounting period. This presents an immediate practical difficulty since, in order to monitor costs effectively for decision-making and control purposes, product costs need to be determined frequently, and not just on an annual basis.

Actual overhead, and actual direct costs or hours, could be collected on a weekly basis. This, however, would be time-consuming and expensive administratively. The process might also be subject to wide seasonal fluctuations and changing application rates which would be difficult to monitor. To overcome both problems *pre-determined* (or *budgeted*) *overhead application rates* are used. Since a rate involves a ratio, budgeted figures are needed for both the numerator and the denominator of that ratio, i.e. for both the total overhead cost to be absorbed, and the measure of activity (in direct labour hours, direct labour costs, etc.) respectively. At the end of the accounting period differences may appear between overhead applied, and actual overhead incurred. When actual overhead is greater (less) than applied overhead the difference is called *under-* (*over-*) *applied overhead.*

Obviously the size of the difference will depend upon the accuracy with which the total overhead costs and the denominator activity volume are forecast.

5.10 Over- and under-applied overhead

Small differences between actual overhead and applied overhead can be dealt with very simply. If the under- (or over-) application is thought to arise from seasonal variations which might cancel out, the difference would normally be carried forward to the next accounting period. If, however, the difference arises in the accounting period for specific reasons which are unlikely to be repeated, the difference would be incorporated in the period's profit and loss account.

Large under- (or over-) applications of overhead can only be due to errors in budgeting. Such errors may be unavoidable: factory accidents, machine breakdowns, failures in raw materials supplies are all possible causes. On the other hand, errors may arise through careless budgeting, production inefficiencies, or failure to recognise changing patterns of costs. In every case, the cause of the error warrants careful investigation. From a costing viewpoint large errors may be *pro-rated* as follows:

Budgeted manufacturing overhead	£150,000
Budgeted activity in direct labour hours (DLH)	30,000
Overhead application rate/DLH	£5
Actual activity (in DLH)	25,000
Overhead applied	£125,000
Actual overhead	£160,000
Under-applied overhead	£35,000

Now suppose:

Closing work-in-progress (in DLH)	1,500
Finishing goods inventory (in DLH)	6,000
Cost of goods sold (in DLH)	10,000

Then the under-applied overhead of £35,000 is pro-rated across work-in-progress, finished goods inventory, and cost of goods sold in the proportions 1,500:6,000:10,000, i.e. £3,000, £12,000, £20,000.

Finally, it should be noted that small application errors – or even none at all – may conceal inaccurate estimates of both the numerator and the denominator in the absorption ratio.

Exercises

1. Outline four different methods for overhead absorption, stating clearly the advantages and disadvantages of each and indicating the most appropriate circumstances in which each could be used.

2. Explain the methods available for the apportionment of service department costs, and indicate the advantages of each.

3. Explain carefully what is meant by each of the terms: overhead apportionment, overhead allocation, and overhead absorption, giving examples to illustrate your answer.

4. Calculate the overhead to be apportioned to each Producing Department given the following data:

| | Producing Departments | | | Service departments | | |
	A	B	C	X	Y	Z
Initial apportionment	£18,000	£3,600	£12,000	£2,100	£9,000	£4,500
Service departments						
X	8%	25%	20%	—	13%	34%
Y	70%	15%	5%	5%	—	5%
Z	15%	18%	17%	30%	20%	—

5. Company A manufactures and sells two products, X and Y. The following data relate to indirect manufacturing costs to be allocated to the two products:

Packaging	£12,000
Rental costs of warehouse	£4,000
Salaries of salespersons	£50,000
Ordering and invoicing costs	£15,000

Annual sales of product X are 12,000 units, and of product Y are 9,600. The number of orders for product X which are processed per year is 3,000, whilst the corresponding number for Y is 2,600. On average 1,200 units of X and 1,000 units of Y are held in finished goods inventory.

It is recognised that to sell a unit of product Y requires twice as much effort as it does to sell a unit of product X. Only two thirds of the warehouse space required for storing a unit of X is needed for storing a unit of Y. Packaging costs for a unit of Y are 25% greater than for a unit of X.

Allocate indirect manufacturing costs to products.

6. Apex Ltd. comprises two service departments and two production departments. Direct costs relating to the four departments are as follows:

| | Producing | | Service | |
	Machining	Assembly	Administration	Maintenance
	£	£	£	£
Materials	200,000	70,000	7,000	10,000
Labour	120,000	180,000	60,000	70,000
Overhead	60,000	160,000	30,000	40,000

The following information is also available:

	Machining	Assembly	Administration	Maintenance
Area (sq. metres)	10,000	9,000	2,000	—
Direct labour hours	20,000	25,000	—	14,000

Apportion costs to producing departments by:

(i) The direct method;
(ii) The reciprocal method.

Chapter 6

Marginal costing and marginal analysis

6.1 Introduction

The process of overhead absorption described in Chapter 5 can be used to allocate both fixed and variable components of overhead to cost units. However, there exist two alternative systems for treating the fixed component of manufacturing overhead. Under a *marginal costing system* fixed manufacturing overhead is not allocated to cost units. Instead, it is treated as a period cost and charged to the profit and loss account for the accounting period in which it is incurred. Under an *absorption costing system*, fixed manufacturing overhead is treated as a product cost and charged to cost units. Both marginal and absorption costing systems treat any variable overhead as a product cost, and allocate it to cost units.

6.2 Marginal and absorption costing systems

Consider the following example which illustrates the different treatment of manufacturing overhead under the marginal (sometimes also called *direct* or *variable*) system and the absorption system. We assume that the variable cost/unit in inventory is £8, and fixed manufacturing overhead is absorbed at £4/unit under absorption costing:

	Opening inventory			Closing inventory		
		Marginal	*Absorp-tion*		*Marginal*	*Absorp-tion*
Year	*No. of units*	*Total cost @ £8/unit*	*Total cost @ £12/unit*	*No. of units*	*Total cost @ £8/unit*	*Total cost @ £12/unit*
1	0	0	0	2,500	20,000	30,000
2	2,500	20,000	30,000	3,500	28,000	42,000
3	3,500	28,000	42,000	1,200	9,600	14,400
4	1,200	9,600	14,000	0	0	0

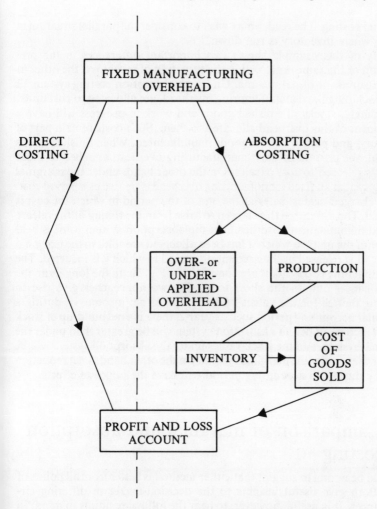

FIG. 20: Flow of fixed manufacturing overhead costs under direct and absorption costing

During year 2, which experiences a build-up of inventory, the value of that inventory increases from £20,000 to £28,000 under marginal costing, and from £30,000 to £42,000 under absorption costing. The increases in inventory value under the two systems are therefore £8,000 and £12,000 respectively. Since £4,000 (i.e. 1,000 extra units at £4 fixed overhead/unit) more costs are retained in inventory under absorption costing, the value for net income under this system must be £4,000 greater than under marginal costing. The reader may wish to consider the parallel situation in year 3, where inventory is run down.

Study of this example shows two important differences in the presentation of the same data: one in the valuation of inventory, the other in the measurement of net income. Under an absorption costing system all costs, including fixed manufacturing overhead, are allocated to cost units. Accordingly, stocks of finished goods and work-in-progress will have a component of this overhead allocated to them. Such costs remain part of inventory, and part of cost of goods manufactured. When finished goods are sold, the portion of fixed manufacturing overhead attached to those goods is released to cost of sales. On the other hand, under the marginal costing system all fixed manufacturing overhead is treated as a period cost, and is charged against sales at the end of the period in which the cost is incurred. The difference then is seen to arise from the timing of the release of fixed manufacturing overhead. In the absorption system some is held back until the units to which it has been allocated are sold: in the marginal system all is released in the accounting period in which it is incurred. The flows under the two systems are compared in Fig. 20. In the long term, the effects cancel out. In the short term, the two approaches give rise to differing figures for the values of stock and of net income. If, during a particular accounting period such as year 2, there is a net build-up of stock the net income under an absorption system will be greater than under the marginal system, and the stock values under the absorption system will be greater than under the marginal system. On the other hand, a net reduction in stock during an accounting period will have the opposite effects.

6.3 Comparison of marginal and absorption costing

It would be wrong to suggest that either method is better from all points of view. Both give useful insights to the decision-maker in differing circumstances. It is useful, however, to bear the following points in mind. In pricing decisions it could be argued that the marginal approach, by excluding fixed manufacturing costs from products, gives a more meaningful basis for arriving at a selling price. Certainly in a situation where, for example, a special order for additional products is received, the marginal costing system is more useful in providing a figure at which goods might be sold in order to recover variable costs. However, the danger is that a unique situation sets a precedent for a future selling price policy which, if adopted, will not cover fixed costs. An absorption system does make it clear what average production cost per unit needs to be covered by the selling price. Under an absorption system it is the case that, when sales are not buoyant and stocks may be building up, the profit figure – by not taking account of all fixed costs for the period – may be overstated. Similarly, under a marginal costing system it is possible that losses may be recorded in an accounting period where, for seasonal reasons, items are being deliberately held in stock for sale in a later period. Naturally, of course, a marginal system avoids the difficulties in budgeting and absorbing fixed manufacturing overhead, and the problems of its over- and under-absorption.

Study of Fig. 20 and the data in §6.2 confirms that the difference in net income under the two systems is just the net increase (or decrease) in numbers of units in inventory, multiplied by the fixed manufacturing overhead to be absorbed per unit.

6.4 Marginal (or contribution) analysis

6.4.1 The approach

The key element in applying marginal costing is the separation of overhead costs into fixed and variable components. The separation of costs into fixed and variable parts also forms the basis of the technique of *marginal* (or *contribution*) *analysis*, which is concerned with budgeting and future profit-planning.

6.4.2 Cost-volume-profit (or break-even) analysis

This is best discussed with a specific example in mind.

Suppose the total costs associated with the manufacture of a particular product comprise £2,000 fixed, and £3.40 variable cost/unit, and that the selling price per unit is £5. Thus, if 1,000 units are produced in, say, a month, and all are sold the costs will be £5,400. The company, therefore, is making and selling the product at a loss of £400 per month. However, if 1,500 units are produced and sold, total costs will be £7,100 and revenue £7,500, indicating a profit of £400. Assuming a constant selling price, the situation is illustrated in Fig. 21, in which both total costs and sales revenue are measured along the vertical axis.

The straight line OA has a gradient equal to the selling price per unit, i.e. £5. Line BC on the other hand commences, when production is zero, at the level of fixed costs. It has a gradient equal to the variable cost/unit of production. The point D, where the two lines representing total sales revenue and total costs respectively intersect, has particular significance. It is known as the *break-even point*. The level of production at this point, i.e. 1,250 units, is that at which revenue and total costs are equal. At lower

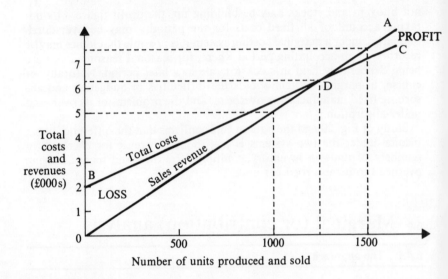

FIG. 21: **Break-even (Cost-Volume-Profit) analysis**

levels of production, e.g. 1,000 units, the total costs exceed revenue, and the *loss* is given by the vertical distance between the two lines. On the other hand, at higher levels of output revenue exceeds total costs by an amount equal to the *profit*. This simple analysis provides an estimate of the minimum level of production necessary to make a profit on the product. It is perhaps worth noting that OA and BC will intersect only if the gradient of OA exceeds that of BC. This is sensible, since the two gradients respectively represent the price/unit and the variable cost – or the marginal cost – of producing a unit. Unless sales price exceeds marginal cost it will be impossible to realise a profit at any production level.

6.4.3 Limitations of CVP analysis

Although useful, the previous analysis has to be used with care. It is based upon several assumptions, some of which are obvious and others not so obvious. They include:

   (i) constant selling price;
   (ii) constant level of fixed costs throughout the range of production levels;
   (iii) all production is always sold;

(iv) variable costs depend linearly on volume produced (i.e. they are exactly proportional to volume);
 (v) all costs are capable of being classified as either fixed or variable;
(vi) only one product is under consideration;
(vii) costs of materials, labour, and so on remain unchanged;
(viii) productivity, technology, and efficiency remain unchanged;
(ix) volume of production is the only factor affecting costs and revenues.

In practice none of these assumptions is likely to be strictly valid. However, over certain ranges and under particular conditions they may be approximately true, and therefore enable the analysis to be used.

6.4.4 Contribution margin

The previous analysis enables the usual income statement to be restated in the format of a *marginal income statement*, particularly useful for planning purposes. The simplest way to illustrate the alternative format is through an example:

Normal format:

Sales		£500,000
less cost of goods sold		300,000
Gross profit		200,000
less Selling and Admin. expenses		100,000
Net profit (Income)		£100,000

Marginal format:

Sales		£500,000
less variable costs		
Manufacturing	£175,000	
Selling and Admin.	75,000	250,000
Contribution margin		£250,000
less Fixed costs		
Manufacturing	£125,000	
Selling and Admin.	25,000	150,000
Net Profit (Income)		£100,000

In this illustration the *contribution margin* is £250,000. It represents the excess of sales revenue over variable costs, and therefore the contribution towards fixed costs and to profits. It may be expressed either as a *total figure*, as a *contribution per unit produced*, or as a *contribution ratio*. It provides a simple way of determining whether a product is profitable or not and of comparing the profitability of different products. By dividing the contribution per unit into the fixed costs figure we are able to determine the number of units necessary to be produced and sold in order to cover fixed costs (i.e. we are able to find easily the break-even production level). Thus, in the illustration of §6.4.2 the contribution per unit is £1.60 (i.e. £5 –

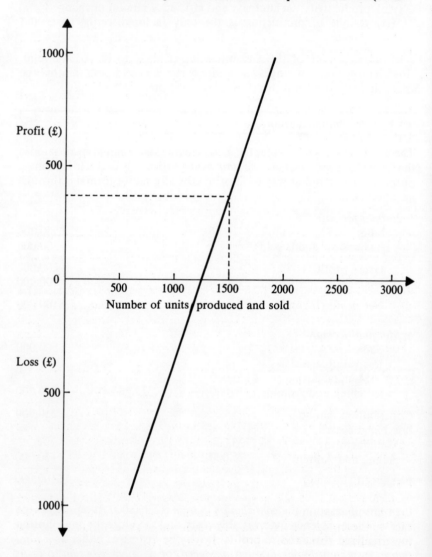

FIG. 22: Profit-volume graph

£3.40). Since fixed costs are £2,000, the number of units produced and sold for break-even is 2,000/1.60 = 1,250 units.

Similarly, the production volume necessary to generate a particular required target profit can be calculated by dividing the contribution ratio into the sum of fixed costs and required profit. Suppose profits of £1,600 are planned, then the number of units to be produced and sold is (2,000 + 1,600)/1.6 = 2,250 units.

6.4.5 Profit-volume charts

As an alternative to the CVP (or break-even) charts, the analysis may be presented in the form of a *profit-volume chart*. Here the vertical axis is used to plot profit, rather than total sales and total costs. The production volume produced and sold remains plotted along the horizontal axis. Using the data of the preceding example, the profit-volume chart would therefore appear as in Fig. 22. As before we note, for example, that the profit is £400 when volume is 1,500 units.

6.5 Determination of cost functions

6.5.2 Graphical analysis

The CVP chart of Fig. 21 illustrates a perfect relationship between costs and revenues on the one hand and production volume on the other. Such a relationship is unlikely to occur in practice, and it is often necessary to estimate a relationship between the factors from observed data. A typical situation is shown in the *scatter graph* or *scatter diagram* of Fig. 23. At least two methods are available.

6.5.2 High-low method

This involves taking the two extreme observed points of the activity range and drawing the straight line XY between them. This assumed linear relationship is then used to predict total costs for intermediate (and as yet unobserved) activity levels. The crudity of this approach is well illustrated in Fig. 23, where considerable differences between predicted and actual future values are likely. For example, the predicted cost at an activity level of 3,500 units is from the "high-low" line, about £26,000. Examination of the whole scatter of points suggests that line AB might give a better overall "fit" to the data points and that a cost estimate of about £23,000 might be more realistic. Part of the failure (and simplicity) of the high-low method is due to the use of only two data points: the remaining data are ignored.

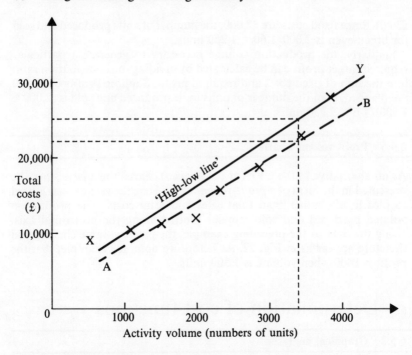

FIG. 23: **High-low method of estimating cost behaviour functions**

6.5.3 Linear regression

The second method takes account of all observed values. It enables calculation of the line which – of all the possible lines which can be drawn on the graph – fits the data in the "best" way. Known as the *regression line*, its *gradient* (m) and its *intercept* (c) on the vertical axis are calculated from the formulae:[1]

$$m = \frac{n \Sigma xy - (\Sigma x)\,(\Sigma y)}{n\,\Sigma x^2 - (\Sigma x)^2}$$

$$c = (\Sigma y - m\Sigma x)/n)$$

Here n is the number of data points (x, y); Σx, Σy, Σx^2 are the sums of the x-values, y-values, and squares of the x-values respectively.

---

[1] For derivation of these formulae see any basic statistics text.

It is not the purpose of this text to derive mathematical formulae. However, the application is illustrated below in a numerical example, which uses information concerning the weekly production and associated costs incurred by Raven & Glass Ltd. in the manufacture of jaggers:

Week	Output of jaggers (X)	Total costs (Y) in £00's	XY	X²
1	2	5.60	11.20	4
2	3	7.80	23.40	9
3	5	10.15	50.75	25
4	4	10.40	41.60	16
5	1	3.90	3.90	1
6	3	5.30	15.90	9
7	2	6.15	12.30	4
8	4	10.75	43.00	16
9	5	11.00	55.00	25
10	6	13.80	82.80	36
Total	35	84.85	339.85	145

$$m = \frac{10\,(339.85) - (35)\,(84.85)}{10\,(145) - (35)^2}$$

$$= 428.75/225 = 1.906$$

$$c = \frac{(84.85) - 1.906\,(35)}{10}$$

$$= 1.816$$

The data are shown in Fig. 24 on p. 78, together with the line of best fit, AB. As an approximation it is possible to interpret the value of c as the fixed costs, and the gradient m as the variable costs/unit.

Exercises

1. Explain the meaning of *marginal costing* and *contribution*. Discuss the advantages and disadvantages of marginal costing.

2. Discuss the suggestion that together direct and absorption costing provide information not given by either method on its own.

3. "Variable (direct) costing gives more useful information for decision-making purposes than does absorption costing." Discuss.

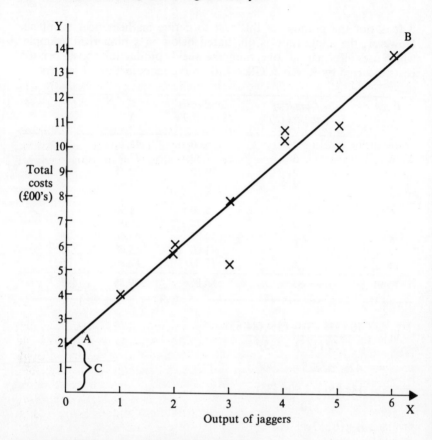

FIG. 24: **Simple linear regression analysis of costs**

4. Discuss clearly the assumptions, limitations, uses, and objectives of cost-volume-profit (break-even) analysis.

5. The following data relate to Shifting Sands Ltd. over the last four years:

	Sales	Profit	Units produced
1982	£340,000	£75,000	3,350
1983	380,000	97,000	3,900
1984	260,000	32,000	2,540
1985	320,000	63,000	3,210

Compute:

(i) Marginal contribution/unit;
(ii) Break-even point (in units);

6. Barrels Ltd. has just taken over the smaller company, Locks and Stocks Ltd. The latter has in recent years manufactured two products only, locks and stocks, in equal volumes.

The chief accountant of Barrels Ltd. has collected the following information relating to the past year's operations of Locks and Stocks. During that year the factory operated at full capacity, as measured in direct machine hours.

	Locks	Stocks
Sales (units)	1,020	1,020
Selling price/unit	£11.50	£12.75
Manufacturing costs:		
Direct materials/unit	£2.25	£1.73
Direct labour/unit	£0.50	£0.50
Variable overhead/unit	£0.52	£1.05
Fixed overhead/unit	£1.49	£1.49

The hourly wage rate for direct labour is £1, and direct labour hours are used as the basis for applying fixed overhead. Direct machine hours form the basis for applying variable overhead. Administrative and selling costs comprise a variable component of £1,050 and a fixed component of £3,100.

Calculate the overall contribution margin and the overall contribution margin ratio for Locks and Stocks last year. Calculate the breakeven point, measured in units, assuming equal numbers of locks and stocks are sold. If profits are to be increased by 30% what sales volume would be needed? Would you recommend that locks and stocks should continue to be marketed in equal volumes? Explain clearly.

7.	Month	Output (units)	Total costs (£000's)
	1	683	164
	2	1,639	221
	3	1,503	205
	4	1,366	191
	5	1,230	197
	6	1,366	204
	7	1,776	217
	8	956	164
	9	820	175
	10	956	178
	11	1,161	166
	12	615	148

The above data refer to twelve months' manufacturing by Kilronan Enterprises.

(a) By plotting the data on a graph estimate variable and fixed costs.
(b) Using regression analysis calculate alternative estimates of these two quantities.

Comment on the usefulness of this analysis of total costs.

8. Uno Ltd. manufactures only one product, solos. During the last year it has produced and sold 50,000 solos at a selling price of £16 each. Contribution margin per solo is £4.

Currently break-even takes place at 55% of sales. It is predicted that demand will be unaffected by a price increase of 9%, but that a price increase of 12% would cause an 8% reduction in demand (measured in units).

Which policy with regard to price change should the company adopt in order to increase its profitability? Explain carefully.

9. Eine Ltd. manufactures a single product, kleins. The following data refer to last year's production and sales:

Sales	121,000
Selling price/unit	£6.70
Fixed costs	£200,000
Variable costs/unit	£4

In order to increase Eine's profitability two policies are under review. The first involves a reduction in selling price to £6 per unit, and in variable costs to £3.70. Sales volume is expected to increase then to 175,000 units although fixed costs would also increase to an estimated £230,000.

A second policy involves no changes in cost structure other than spending a further £13,500 on advertising during the coming year. As a direct result sales (in numbers of units) are forecast to increase by 24%.

You are required to make recommendations to management – supported by a clear analysis – of which, if any, of the new policies should be adopted.

Chapter 7

Cost accounting systems

7.1 Types of systems

For simplicity we have assumed in Chapters 5 and 6 that large numbers of similar, distinct product units were being manufactured. The individual units of product were the ultimate cost units to which direct and indirect manufacturing costs were charged. We now need to recognise that many manufacturing activities are not of this type. In the construction industry, for example, a building contractor may be working on three quite different projects on different building sites. Alternatively, a customer may place a special order with a manufacturer for the production of a number of specific goods. Fortunately, many of the concepts introduced previously can still be used, although it is necessary to modify some of the procedures.

For convenience, cost accounting systems may be divided into two major types: *operations costing systems* and *specific order costing systems*.

The first is appropriate when a repetitive series of operations or processes is taking place. The result is a fairly continuous output of uniform *goods* or *services*. Costs are charged to units of output by averaging total costs over numbers of output units produced. Examples include the manufacture of light-bulbs, and the service provided by a hair-dresser. The second system is used when the output takes the form of specific, separate jobs, contracts, or batches. Costs are allocated to the specific order with which they can be identified. An example would be the contract to build a new hospital. The similarities and differences between the two systems are made clear in the following sections. For convenience, each system is broken down into further sub-classifications.

7.2 Operations costing systems

7.2.1 Process costing

In the definition of §7.1 reference was made to the provision of goods or services. Process costing is used when goods are being manufactured in a standard way. The products are not made to meet a particular customer's needs. Instead, they are mass-produced, on a continuous basis, to a set design. Many everyday goods are made in this way: cutlery, books, tins of food, packets of sugar, are all common examples.

Under such a system it is impossible to identify costs uniquely with product units. Instead, an averaging of total costs across units produced is necessary to arrive at a *cost per unit*. Unfortunately, in practice this is not quite so simple as it sounds. A typical production process involves several stages. The raw materials and partly finished goods move steadily from one stage to another, whilst different operations are carried out on them. The output from one stage forms the input to the next, where additional raw materials may be added or labour employed. Because of the continuous nature of the process, at any time some units of product will be incomplete. A motor-car production line provides a simple illustration: at any time some vehicles will be almost complete, others only just commencing manufacture, and others at intermediate stages of production. In general, at the end of a costing period a method is needed of apportioning the costs of operations between *work-in-progress* and *finished goods*. In order to resolve this difficulty we need to introduce the concept of *equivalent units*.

Suppose that at the end of a costing period 100 units are completed, and 50 units remain 20% completed. The *total equivalent output* measured at the end of that period is calculated as 100 + (20% x 50), i.e. 100 + 10 = 110 units. In other words, the 50 units which are estimated to be 20% complete as far as their manufacture is concerned, are treated as equivalent to 10 complete units. Suppose that manufacturing cost of £5,500 were to be allocated to production. Then:

$$\text{Cost/completed unit} = \frac{\text{cost incurred}}{\text{Number of equivalent units produced}}$$

$$= \frac{£5,500}{110}$$

$$= £50/\text{unit}$$

Both cost and number of equivalent units must of course relate to the same costing period.

A further complication in practice is that manufacturing costs are made up of three components, i.e. direct labour, direct materials, and manufacturing overhead. It may well be that partially completed units of production are not completed to the same extent under each cost heading. A unit may be 80% complete as far as direct materials are concerned, but only 40% with respect to manufacturing overhead. To meet this practical difficulty consider the following illustration which relates to a particular production period:

Completed units   :   250 units
Incomplete units   :   110 units
Percentage completion
of work in progress   :   Labour   70%
                                    Materials 65%
                                    Overhead 45%

	Total equivalent units of production	Total costs (£)	Cost/unit
Labour	327 (i.e. 0.70 × 110 + 250)	15,000	45.87
Materials	321.50 (i.e. 0.65 × 110 + 250)	18,500	57.54
Overhead	299.50 (i.e. 0.45 × 110 + 250)	21,000	70.12
	Total	54,500	173.53

Note that the cost to be attached to production completed during the period is:

250 × £173.53 = £43,382.50

and that the cost of *closing work in progress* at the end of the costing period is:

£54,500 – £43,382.50 = £11,117.50

This latter figure can also be derived as:

[(0.70 × 110) × £45.87] + [(0.65 × 110) × £57.54] + [(0.45 × 110) × £70.12] = £11,117.50

Obviously, any closing work-in-progress at the end of one period forms opening work-in-progress at the beginning of the next period. At this point is is useful to consider the manufacturing process as a series of different stages. Stage 2, for example, takes its input from stage 1 and forwards its completed output to stage 3:

We need to distinguish carefully between two types of materials cost as far as stage 2 is concerned. Firstly we have the production output of stage 1, which is 100% finished as far as stage 1 is concerned, but which forms only one of the possible raw materials for stage 2. Secondly, during stage 2 certain other raw materials are added to the product. At the beginning of a costing period unfinished units in stage 2 will have therefore the following costs associated with them:

    (i) Input raw material cost (i.e. finished output from stage 1);
    (ii) Added material cost (in stage 2);
    (iii) Labour cost (in stage 2);
    (iv) Overhead cost (in stage 2).

It is the last three of these which may be incomplete in stage 2 at the beginning (or end) of a costing period. Since input raw material to stage 2 must be completely finished in stage 1 before being transferred to stage 2, the cost of input raw material must be complete as far as all units in stage 2 are concerned, irrespective of whether those units are complete or incomplete with regard to costs (ii), (iii), and (iv) in stage 2.

The objective is to attach costs incurred during a costing period to the production of that period. When there exists opening work-in-progress we need to incorporate the value of that opening work-in-progress into the calculation (see, for example, Fig. 25).

It should be noted, however, that this figure is not the production costs of stage 2 during the costing period. It is the cost at the end of that period of equivalent production to the end of stage 2, including all costs from stage 1, and incorporating figures of both completed production and of closing work-in-progress.

Typically, each stage of manufacture will be designated a process cost centre for cost flow purposes (see Chapter 2). The activities of such a centre over, say, a monthly costing period are summarised in monthly costing reports (see Fig. 25). The flow of costs is depicted in Fig. 26.

In any continuous manufacturing process it is inevitable that not all raw materials are incorporated into the final products. For example, liquid losses occur through evaporation, metal filings are deposited in machining processes, and so on. Some losses of this nature are *avoidable*, some *unavoidable*. Evaporative losses may be largely avoidable through using closed containers for liquids, although the costs of doing so may be greater than the costs of liquid loss. Sawdust and metal filings, however, would be largely unavoidable. The losses deemed unavoidable, given the character of the particular production process, are usually included in the total costs to be averaged across production units. Avoidable costs, however, need to be considered separately, and are themselves split into two components: *normal losses* and *abnormal losses*.

The first recognises that some losses occur through worker error, accident, or breakdown. It is reasonable to include these in total costs for allocation to product units: in other words to spread the costs of "bad" production across the "good" production. However, unusually high avoidable losses require further investigation and remedial action.

RAVEN & GLASS LTD.

PRODUCTION COSTS REPORT
OCTOBER 1985
Painting and Drying Department

NUMBERS OF UNITS

Units to be accounted for:

Opening work-in-progress, 1 October	2500	
Transfers in from previous department during October	7800	10300

Units accounted for:

Transfers out to next department during October	8200	
Closing work-in-progress, 31 October	2100	10300

COSTS

	Cost	No. of equivalent units	Cost/unit
Costs to be accounted for:			
(a) Opening work-in-progress:			
Previous department	£10,000	2500	£4.00
Direct materials	4,830	2300	2.10
Direct labour	3,500	1400	2.50
Factory overhead	3,360	1400	2.40
(b) Production in October:			
Previous department	£31,980	7800	£4.10
Direct materials	18,275	8500	2.15
Direct labour	18,144	7200	2.52
Factory overhead	17,568	7200	2.44
	£107,657		
Costs accounted for:			
(a) Transfers out to next department during October:			
Previous department	£10,000	2500	£4.00
	23,370	5700	4.10
Direct materials	4,830	2300	2.10
	12,685	5900	2.15
Direct labour	3,500	1400	2.50
	17,136	6800	2.52
Factory overhead	3,360	1400	2.40
	16,592	6800	2.44
(b) Closing work-in-progress:			
Previous department	£8,610	2100	£4.10
Direct materials	5,590	2600	2.15
Direct labour	1,008	400	2.52
Factory overhead	976	400	2.44
	£107.657		

FIG. 25: **Monthly production costs report**

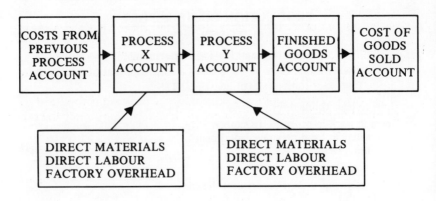

FIG. 26: **Flow of costs through process accounts**

Naturally, what constitutes abnormal loss and what normal depends upon experience and the specific process.

7.2.2 By-products and joint products

It is quite common in a continuous manufacturing process to find that more than one product may result from the initial processing of raw materials. An obvious example is the petrochemicals industry where, by fractional distillation, input of crude oil results in the manufacture of a wide variety of products. A distinction can be made between two categories of such products: *by-products* and *joint products*. It must be emphasised, however, that the distinction is a matter of judgement. Classification may vary between accountants and between industries.

Basically by-products are seen as products arising incidentally alongside the manufacture of the main product. As such they are products of sufficient value not to be classified as *waste* or *scrap*. It would not be sensible therefore simply to discard them. Nevertheless, they do not form a very significant component of the total saleable value of goods produced. In other words, if the main thrust of the manufacturing process is to produce certain products, but in so doing a further saleable product is inevitably produced, then the latter would normally be defined as a by-product. For example, a sawmill will produce wooden planks as a main product. In doing so, a significant quantity of sawdust and woodchips are produced. If these are sold for agricultural and horticultural purposes they would normally be seen as a by-product.

Joint products, on the other hand, are those which have similar saleable values at the end of the production process, but which nevertheless arise from the same original input of the raw materials. Returning to our sawmill illustration, in addition to planks of standard length there will be many of smaller sizes. If these are sold to a furniture manufacturer these might be seen as a joint-product.

In the cases of both joint- and by-products it is possible to identify a stage in the production process known as the *split-off point*. Beyond this

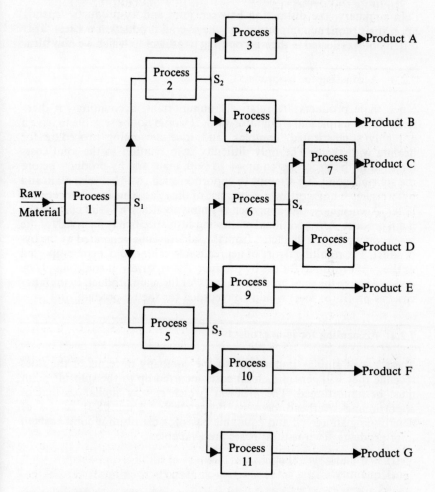

FIG. 27: **Complex manufacturing process involving multiple joint products and split-off points (S_1, S_2, S_3, S_4)**

point, initial processing of raw materials ceases to be common to all products. Both joint- and by-products will normally require distinct processing, and perhaps different inputs of additional raw materials, beyond the split-off point. In complex processes, such as occur in the petrochemicals industry, there may well be several identifiable split-off points giving rise to a range of joint (and, indeed, by-) products. In Fig. 27, for example, seven joint products result from a sequence of eleven processes each involving unique additions of raw materials. Four split-off points – S_1, S_2, S_3, S_4 – can be identified.

In summary, the distinction between joint and by-products depends upon their economic importance in the overall production process. This difference is reflected in their accounting treatment to which we now turn.

7.2.3 Accounting for by-products

Since these products are relatively unimportant, accounting for them needs to be simple and straightforward. It would not be sensible to have a a highly sophisticated, complex, and time-consuming procedure for dealing with them. The only difficulty is in relation to the joint costs incurred in the processes common to both main and by-products before the split-off point. To attempt to apportion such costs between main and by-products is not worthwhile, because of the relative insignificance of the latter. Accordingly, one approach is simply to attach all joint costs to the main product. Any additional processing costs specifically incurred for the by-product are then deducted from the sales revenue generated by the by-product. The resulting figure of net realisable value could then be reported as the profit (or loss) for the by-product. Alternatively, it could simply be deducted from the total production costs for the main product. In the latter case no profit (or loss) would be recorded for the by-product.

7.2.4 Accounting for joint products

These are of similar importance to the company in terms of the sales revenue they will generate. Joint costs incurred up to the split-off point must be apportioned. The problem (which is very similar to that of apportioning overhead between departments – see §5.3) is one of determining an agreed and equitable basis for distributing joint costs to joint products. Two natural bases are available:

(i) net realisable value;
(ii) quantity.

In the first of these, joint costs incurred up to the split-off point are apportioned on the basis of sales revenue from each product less the processing and other costs attributable to that product beyond split-off. The second, however, apportions the joint costs in proportion to the quantity of joint material present in each of the final products. (Note that it is not the quantities of end-product which are used, since beyond split-off different raw materials will typically be added to different products.)

The following examples illustrate the two approaches when joint costs up to split-off are £80,000:

(i)

	Product		Total
	A	B	
Sales (£)	250,000	400,000	650,000
Costs after split-off (£)	100,000	300,000	400,000
Difference (£)	150,000	100,000	250,000
Apportionment of joint costs incurred before split-off (£)	48,000	32,000	80,000

(ii) If joint material (up to split-off) is present in final products A and B in proportions 3:5 respectively, then joint costs of £80,000 would be apportioned as:

A : $\frac{3}{8} \times £80,000 = £30,000$
B : $\frac{5}{4} \times £80,000 = £50,000$

Neither method can be described as "right" or "wrong": which to use is a matter of judgement.

7.2.5 Service costing systems

Two types of operations costing systems can be identified. We have discussed process costing at length: *service costing* can be dealt with briefly. It is appropriate where a standard form of service is provided. A service cost centre – such as computing – may provide such a service to other cost centres within the organisation, or sometimes to clients outside the organisation. Alternatively, an organisation may provide a standard service to outside customers only. Airline operators, hospitals, and educational institutions would fall into this category.

Under such a system the cost per unit is defined simply by:

$$\frac{\text{Total costs during the costing period}}{\substack{\text{Total number of service units processed} \\ \text{during the costing period}}}$$

The only difficulty is in finding a suitable service unit. In the case of the airline it might be a passenger-mile, of the hospital a patient-day, of an educational institution a pupil-week.

7.3 Specific order costing systems

7.3.1 Job costing

Normally a job costing system is used when the organisation carries out work in response to specific orders from its customers. In other words, each job is clearly different from all others, and is therefore identifiable as a cost unit. The job remains identifiable as a single cost unit throughout the work processes which are performed on it. As an example, a motor vehicle repairer would operate a job costing system, since each individual car is clearly identifiable, and will need different work doing to it. One car may need a new exhaust, another may need repairs to the steering, another the brakes.

When an order is received from a customer and accepted, the first step is for the production control department to issue a *production order*. This gives a complete, detailed, specification of what is to be made, or what is to be done. Each production order will have a serial number by which it can be uniquely identified. Within the accounting department a *job cost sheet*, or *job cost card*, or *job cost account*, again identified by a unique *job number* is created in order to record all costs associated with the specific job. This job number is used on time-sheets, for example, when work is performed on that job. The number is also used on all requisitions of materials from stores, and on purchase orders. Overhead is entered on the job cost sheet using predetermined overhead absorption rates. A typical job cost sheet is shown in Fig. 28.

Since the cost of a job is clearly identified, calculation of profit on a job is very straightforward. All we need do is compare this cost with the price charged to the customer. Furthermore, original estimates provided to the customer prior to accepting the job can be compared with the job cost account to reveal efficiencies and inefficiencies, and to provide a guide to better estimation in the future. As the job progresses through the system, costs are collected and identified with that job. It may be that in doing so costs may arise from different accounting periods. This will depend upon the nature of the job. If, for example, the job is to meet an order for an item of custom-built furniture then costs from two different accounting periods are unlikely to be charged to the job. If, however, the job is a contract for the construction of a building, then it is more than likely that the job may extend over more than one accounting period (see §7.3.3). Entries on the job cost card will give rise to debit entries in the work-in-progress account,

RAVEN & GLASS LTD.				
JOB COST SHEET				

Job No: _____ Date started: _____
Job Description: _____ Date completed: _____
Customer: _____ Date promised: _____
Customer ref: _____

Ref. No.	Date		ACTUAL COST	ESTIMATED COST
		Direct materials:		
		Sub-total		
		Direct labour:		
		Sub-total		
		Direct expenses:		
		Sub-total		
		Manufacturing overhead:		
		Sub-total		
		Total manufacturing costs:		

FIG. 28: **Typical job-cost sheet**

and matched credit entries in, for example, the wages payable account, the raw materials inventory account, and the manufacturing overhead account. When the job has been completed, the production control department informs the accounting department. All appropriate remaining costs are charged to the job cost account which is then closed. The figure for total cost recorded on the job cost sheet can be credited to the work-in-progress account, and debited to the finished goods inventory account. The final step when the completed job is sold, will then be the crediting of finished goods and the debiting of cost of goods sold.

7.3.2 Batch costing

It is quite common for a manufacturer to receive a specific order for a number of identical items. For example, a clothing manufacturer may be asked to produce 100 dresses of a specific design for a retailer. Although it would be difficult to identify costs with each dress, the order itself is a specific, identifiable order to which costs can easily be attached. This situation is an example where *batch costing* is appropriate. The only difference between this and job costing, is that when the job (i.e. batch) is completed, and all costs attributable to the batch have been entered on the cost sheet, a unit cost per item can be calculated by dividing total job cost by the number of items in the batch.

7.3.3 Contract costing

Both job costing and batch costing usually involve jobs of relatively short duration. However, there are other types of job which – although readily identifiable, and therefore suitable for a specific order costing system – may extend over a long period of time. A common characteristic of this type of job is that it is not carried out at the organisation's own premises. A good example is the construction industry where a builder may have a contract to build a new hospital over a three-year period.

The system of *contract costing*, designed to deal with this type of situation, has many of the characteristics of job costing since obviously a unique, identifiable "job" exists to which costs can be charged. There are, however, a number of distinctive features. Firstly contracts are often on a large scale, involving considerable resources and a variety of activities. Consequently, contracts are often broken down into smaller jobs, or *subcontracts*. The main contractor for the hospital, for example, may subcontract the equipping of operating theatres to a firm specialising in such work, and the installation of water and heating systems to a plumbing firm. In addition to the identification number given to the main contract, each sub-contract also has a number assigned to it. Costs relating to each sub-contract are recorded on a cost sheet for that sub-contract, and are summarised on a cost sheet for the main contract. The main contract cost sheet plays a role similar to that of the work-in-progress account in the job/batch costing systems.

Many costs normally classified as overhead become direct costs under a contract costing system. One reason for this is the large size of a typical contract. A second reason is that, since the site is distant from the firm's premises, it has a separate identity. The provision of services – water, gas, electricity – to the site would be a direct cost of the contract. Any professional legal, engineering, or architectural fees relating to the contract would be charged to the contract as direct costs. Again, costs of supervisory labour and administrative staff on-site would form part of the direct-labour costs of the contract. As a result, the overhead to be absorbed by a contract is often very small.

There are two ways of dealing with the costs of the plant and machinery used in carrying out a contract. The first involves valuation of the plant before and after use on the contract. If plant is purchased specifically for use on the contract, and has no value when the contract is complete the purchase cost would be charged to the contract as a direct cost. Suppose, however, that the plant has already been in use on other contracts beforehand and may be used on other contracts afterwards. In such circumstances the *written-down values* (i.e. purchase price less depreciation) at the beginning and end of the contract period would be used. The difference between these values (i.e. the depreciation figure for the period) would be charged to the contract.

As an alternative method, hire charges for plant can be made to a contract. For example, if trucks from the company's central fleet are used on the contract, by keeping a record of their times of use and applying an hourly hire rate a suitable charge can be calculated. Care needs to be taken in setting the hourly rate since this needs to cover depreciation, fuel and other running costs, maintenance, operators' wages and so on. On the other hand, if inefficiency is to be avoided attention also needs to be given to external competitive hire charges.

Because of the long-term nature of most contract work it is not feasible for the main contractor to wait until completion of the contract before receiving any payment. Without *interim* or *progress payments* he would not be able to pay wages, materials, and other regularly occurring costs. The timing of such payments is built into the contract, and their value based upon valuation of the incomplete contract at pre-determined times. These valuations are based upon invoices produced by the contractor and validated by an *architect's certificate*. Usually, however, progress payments are not paid immediately in full. Some part – perhaps 5% or 10% – is held back as *retention money*, to be paid say three or six months later when any defects which might emerge in the interim have been rectified.

A final, unique feature of contract costing relates to *profit calculation*. Since contracts may extend over several years it is not practical to calculate a profit figure only when the contract is complete. To do so would distort the financial statements in the preceding years when no profit was recognised. On the other hand, traditional accountancy conservatism is reluctant to recognise profits which have not been realised. As a compromise, normal practice is to base annual profit figures upon the value of certificated work. The details vary, but the following illustration is fairly typical:

$$\text{Profit estimated} = \frac{2}{3} \times \text{notional profit} \times \frac{\text{cash received}}{\text{value of certificated work}}$$

Thus, if:

Cost to date	=	£150,000
Value of certified work	=	£230,000
Cash received	=	£207,000

$$\text{Profit estimated} = \frac{2}{3} \times (230{,}000 - 150{,}000) \times \frac{207{,}000}{230{,}000}$$

$$= £48{,}000$$

Three points are worth noting. Firstly the factor:

$$\frac{\text{cash received}}{\text{value of certificated work}}$$

is introduced to make some allowance for the retention money. If, for example, retention is 10% this factor will have a value of 0.90. Secondly, the *notional profit* is the difference between the value of certificated work to date, and the cost of that work. Thirdly, the factor of 2/3 introduces an element of *conservatism*, since the profit is not actually realised and some provision needs to be made for unanticipated future problems.

When work on a contract is well advanced it is possible that remaining future costs can be accurately estimated. Expected profit can therefore be estimated reasonably precisely by subtracting estimated total costs from the known contract price. This figure for expected profit can be apportioned between the period from start of work to the present, and the period from present to date of expected completion. The basis for apportionment could be the cost of work to date, and the estimated total cost. Alternatively, one could use value of certificated work to date, and total contract price. The following illustrates the procedure.

Suppose a contract is expected to be completed at the end of year 4. It is now the end of year 3, and costs of work to date are £3M. Estimated future costs are £0.6M. The contract price is £5.2M. Expected profit is therefore £5.2M – £3.6M = £1.6M. Estimated profit to date can be calculated as

$3/3.6 \times £1.6M = £1.33M$, and estimated profit in year 4 as $0.6/3.6 \times £1.6M = £0.27M$. Again, in the interests of conservatism these profit figures might be subject to a reducing factor.

Exercises

1. Outline the general circumstances in which you would expect a process costing system to be used. Give three examples.

2. Common costs associated with a common manufacturing process, and incurred up to the point of separation, need to be apportioned. Discuss critically, with examples, the methods which are available.

3. Compare and contrast the problems of analysis and control of costs in a job costing system and a process costing system.

4. What are the objectives you would seek to achieve in developing a cost accounting system?

5. Define clearly the following:

   (i) Joint product;
   (ii) By-product;
   (iii) Point of separation.

6. "It is meaningless to use the term 'true cost' in relation to a product, since every costing exercise involves individual judgement at some stage." Discuss, with examples.

7. Explain, in detail, with appropriate examples, the operation of a contract costing system.

8. "Although contract costing and job costing are both concerned with attaching profits and costs to specific 'orders', there are many differences between the two systems." Discuss.

9. Blanco Ltd. manufactures a wide range of household cleaners and detergents. The market is competitive. Discuss the approach you would make in developing a cost system which would enable you to control advertising costs and evaluate their effectiveness.

10. Alban Ltd. uses a process costing system. An average cost basis is used for tracing costs. Calculate the number of equivalent units manufactured in each of the following *independent* sets of circumstances.

(i) On 1 January Dept. Beta had 8,000 units in process, and these were $\frac{2}{3}$ completed with respect to work in Dept. Beta. It transferred out 32,000

96 · Cost accounting systems

units to Dept. Gamma during January, and received in from Dept. Alpha 40,000 units during the same period. On 31 January all units in Dept. Beta were $\frac{9}{10}$ completed with respect to work in Dept. Beta.

(ii) On 1 March Dept. Sigma had 21,000 units in process, and these units were $\frac{5}{7}$ complete with respect to work in Dept. Sigma. During March, 90,000 units were received from Dept. Rho, and 70,000 units were transferred out to Dept. Tau. On 30 March all units in Dept. Sigma were $\frac{1}{4}$ complete with respect to work in Dept. Sigma.

11. Omega Ltd., which commenced operations on 1 January, manufactures two joint products (kappas and lambdas) and one by-product (iotas) from one raw material input. The following data are available for the month of January:

	Sales (kg)	Production (kg)	Selling prices (£/kg)
Kappas	8,209	8,955	4.45
Lambdas	5,224	5,970	2.22
Iotas	1,493	1,493	0.64

In addition there was 746kg of waste, having no value. This was viewed as normal wastage. Production costs were as follows:

Materials (17,164 kg @ £1.75/kg)	£21,884
Labour	£13,335
Overhead	£15,240

Calculate two sets of values for the overall gross profit, and the gross profit for kappas and lambdas separately, by using two different bases for allocating joint costs.

Chapter 8

Budgeting

8.1 Definitions

Three new terms will be used frequently in this chapter. *Budgeting* is the process of preparing detailed financial plans concerning the future operations of the company. The plans, which may be over the short term (say months) or over the long term (years) are presented in a numerical form involving monetary sums. These plans are called *budgets*. The process of *budgetary control* involves the monitoring of actual company activities and their comparison with predetermined budgets. When actual events depart from those budgeted, budgetary control is also concerned with taking necessary steps to return to the plan, or to modify the plan.

8.2 Objectives of budgeting

In the conduct of our everyday lives we are all familiar with the need to plan our activities. Our plans may include appointments for meetings in the future, organising our personal finances in order that expenditure does not exceed income, or saving for a large item which we are unable to buy now. Without such basic planning our lives would be both very difficult and very inefficient. We would simply waste a great deal of time and effort, and achieve very little.

Business organisations, large or small, likewise require *planning* for future activities and events if they are to survive. In the absence of basic planning the organisation would, for example, have no raw materials when required, inadequate or excessive labour resources, and shortages or an excess of cash. It would produce for sale either products for which there was no demand, or the right product but in either insufficient numbers to meet the demand, or in numbers far in excess of demand and which would therefore be wasted. The need for business planning is obvious. It is also obvious that in order to plan, clear and specific commercial, social, and economic objectives must first be defined. Only then can plans be devised which are consistent with those objectives. To repeat the analogy, it is of little value to have a comfortable, efficient and reliable car but no destination, and no maps. Having determined our destination and drawn the appropriate map to get there we need to be sure that we are going by the route which satisfies our requirements best (i.e. the most scenic, the shortest, or the quickest), and we need to allow for obstacles on the way. These may involve road repairs or accidents, over which we have little control, or they may involve breakdowns by the vehicle, punctures, or running out of fuel or water. The latter are difficulties for which we can plan in advance by carrying spares, and by taking cans of fuel and water.

In exactly the same way, a business organisation needs to allow in its future plans for possible shortages of raw materials, for strikes, for reduced demand, for cash shortages, and so on.

An important function of financial planning, or budgeting, is to *co-ordinate* the various activities of the organisation. This will ensure that all parts of the organisation are working towards the same objectives. Without this *goal congruence* we may find, for example, that the sales department is planning to extend the markets for the company's products when the purchasing department is unable to obtain any more raw materials, or the personnel department is unable to hire additional labour. By analogy again, just as all parts of a car must be working in harmony and be responsive to the driver, so must the activities of different departments and processes be consistent with each other and the overall objectives of the firm.

The required co-ordination is achieved by developing a set of budgets, each of which covers a particular aspect (sales, for example) of the organisation's activities. A *master budget* (see §8.6) then integrates all these *subsidiary budgets* to provide a unified quantitative future plan.

Another major objective of budgeting is to provide control. This relies on the identification of actual deviations from budgets, and the initiation of appropriate action. The latter may involve steps to return operations to budget, or – depending on the reason for the observed deviation – it may involve amendment of plans. Again, in making our journey by car, an accident blocking the road may mean that we have to travel by a different route to reach our destination.

The successful implementation of a budget depends upon people with managerial responsibility taking necessary action. To do this, a manager must understand the budget for which he is responsible, and the way in which it fits into the company's overall plans. Usually this is done through his participation in the preparation of the particular budget. More than that, however, he needs to *communicate* the details of the budget and its significance to the employees whom he supervises. Plans which are misunderstood are unlikely to be carried out properly. Finally, to be achieved most successfully the manager and those he supervises need to believe that his budget is practical and realistic, and should derive satisfaction from its attainment. In other words, the budget must *motivate* those responsible for putting it into practice. Plans which are ambitious (but not unrealistic), which recognise difficulties, which give rewards, and which are practical, are likely to be successfully accomplished. To design budgets needs a great deal of commonsense and understanding by a manager, and a practical knowledge of individual and group behaviour.

8.3 Preparation of budgets

Budgeting, unfortunately, takes place within an environment over which the organisation has only limited control. Thus, little can be done by the firm to change external social, legal, economic, and political forces. Within this, however, a primary concern of top management must be to define its objectives clearly. It must then communicate those objectives to the individual managers responsible for the preparation of budgets. Before the preparation of individual budgets can begin, it is essential that areas of *responsibility* be made absolutely clear. It would not be sensible to have a departmental manager, for example, preparing a budget which included costs attributable to another department. Furthermore, distinctions need to be made between those costs which are *controllable*, and which can therefore properly be made the responsibility of an individual manager, and those which are *uncontrollable*. It would serve no purpose to blame a manager for future deviations between actual and budgeted costs when he had no authority over expenditures in relation to those costs. It is also necessary before budget preparation to ensure that internal accounting systems recognise, and are consistent with, the management structure of authority and responsibility. Finally, it is futile to set budgets which are almost impossible to achieve. Standard costing (see Chapter 9) plays a key rôle in setting cost standards which can be used in budget preparation.

Normally, a *budget officer* is given overall responsibility for the budget process. Although he would not himself prepare individual budgets, he would be responsible for the necessary data collection, and for the administration of the agreed budgets. Typically the company accountant would act as budget officer. He would service a *budget committee*, comprising the senior executives with responsibilities for the operational and financial aspects of the company. The role of this committee is to discuss draft budgets, to recommend modifications as necessary, and to ensure that individual subsidiary budgets are co-ordinated in a manner consistent with overall company objectives.

Budgeting takes place with a particular future period of time in mind. Usually this is one year, although individual budgets may be broken down later into, say, monthly budgets. The process of budgeting is time-consuming and expensive, and it is usually not practical to budget in detail for periods of less than a year. Furthermore, although overall budgets for periods of longer than a year may be considered, it can be very difficult to estimate many of the detailed variables more than a year in advance.

As a basic input to the budgeting process forecasts are obviously needed of, for example, sales, demand, prices of raw materials, and labour costs. Forecasting is a subject in itself, and too complex to cover in this book. We must assume that forecasts are available when needed. Normally, these are based upon historic information, judgement, and statistical analyses of previous trends and cycles.

In preparing budgets it is always tempting to use the previous year's budgets as a starting point. New budgets could be easily prepared, for example, by increasing last year's by a percentage amount equal to the inflation rate. This, however, has the major disadvantage that any sources of inefficiency last year (and which provide opportunities for savings next year) are ignored. It is also not uncommon for those preparing budgets to exaggerate their predicted costs. One reason for doing so would be to gain praise, and perhaps reward, for achieving actual performance well within budget. A second would be to anticipate a revision of the budget downwards by the budget committee.

Zero-base budgeting (ZBB) attempts to avoid both of these problems by insisting that all budget items are justified. Nothing is assumed to be necessary without clear evidence. Although a useful approach every few years, ZBB is a major exercise difficult to implement on an annual basis.

It is impossible in a text of this nature to consider in detail the many behavioural aspects of budgeting and budgetary control. We have mentioned one or two briefly, but for a more thorough discussion the interested reader is referred to, for example, Emmanuel, C.R. and Otley, D.T.: *Accounting for Management Control*, Van Nostrand Reinhold, Wokingham, 1985.

8.4 Limiting factors

In whatever areas of a company a budget is being prepared, there will be a factor which prevents activity exceeding a particular level. For example, production may be limited because no further supplies of raw materials exist, or because of lack of additional labour.

Investment in new plant and equipment may be limited by a ceiling on the amount of bank financing which the company can raise. Such constraints are known as *limiting factors*. Additionally, the organisation overall will be limited in its activities by a particular constraint. This is known as the *principal budget factor* (or *key factor*). It may be one of those constraints already mentioned, although an upper limit on market demand for the company's product often makes sales the principal budget factor.

8.5 Subsidiary budgets

8.5.1 Definitions

Assume that the principal budget factor is the demand for the company's products, and that any necessary forecasts of costs, supplies of materials, labour, and so on have been made.

The process of preparing individual budgets by departments or areas of activity can now begin. Such budgets are known as *subsidiary budgets*. We shall consider a few of these in detail for illustration. However, it must be recognised that subsidiary budgets are needed for each and every aspect of the organisation which involves income or expenditure.

For convenience, subsidiary budgets are classified as follows:

  (i) *Operating budgets*
      These include sales, production, direct materials, direct labour, direct expenses, and overhead;
 (ii) *Administration budget*;
(iii) *Research and development budget*;
 (iv) *Capital expenditure budget*;
  (v) *Cash budget*.

A selection of these is now discussed in more detail.

8.5.2 Operating budgets

The *sales budget* is the responsibility of the chief sales executive. It is his task to prepare for each product a detailed breakdown of likely sales over the budget period. In so doing he will use past sales information, by area and by salesman. He will also use his own judgement in relation to future trends, competition, and changes in the economic, financial, and legal environment outside the firm. His analyses will be in the form of both quantities and prices. Against these he will need to set estimates of sales costs, including salaries and commissions for the required number of salesmen, together with administrative, advertising, marketing and distribution costs in order to arrive at the final sales budget. This budget is perhaps the most important in the budgeting process, since all other subsidiary budgets are related to it. If the sales budget is inaccurate, then so will be the others. A simple sales budget is illustrated below:

Sales budget		
Quarter	No. of units	Sales revenues (£)
Jan – Mar	8,000	48,000
Apr – Jun	7,000	42,000
Jul – Sept	9,000	54,000
Oct – Dec	8,500	51,000

Preparation of the *production budget* by the production manager needs to be consistent with the sales budget, and with current and planned resources. These include raw materials, labour, and plant capacity. This budget will need to be prepared on the basis of each individual product line. It will need to take account of direct labour and direct materials quantities and costs, overhead, efficiency, and the anticipated levels of opening and closing inventories of finished goods and work-in-progress. Although it would usually be ideal to plan production to take place at a uniform rate throughout the budget period, this is difficult to achieve in practice. Demand may fluctuate from one season to another, and supplies of raw materials and labour may vary from month to month. An example of a production budget (in units) is:

Production budget				
Quarter	Opening stock	Production	Sales	Closing stock
Jan – Mar	2,000	9,000	8,000	3,000
Apr – Jun	3,000	6,000	7,000	2,000
July – Sept	2,000	8,000	9,000	1,000
Oct – Dec	1,000	9,000	8,500	1,500

A production cost budget would then give details of expected materials, labour, and overhead costs associated with the above planned production of units.

Following the production budgets, preparation of direct materials, direct labour, direct expenses, cash, and other budgets fall naturally into place. For example:

Direct materials budget (£)				
Quarter	Opening stock	Purchases	Used in production	Closing stock
Jan – Mar	8,000	37,600	36,000	9,600
Apr – Jun	9,600	20,000	24,000	5,600
Jul – Sept	5,600	29,600	32,000	3,200
Oct – Nov	3,200	37,200	36,000	4,400

Here direct materials costs are budgeted at £4/unit, and purchases of direct materials are budgeted at:

Jan – Mar	9400 units
Apr – Jun	5,000 units
Jul – Sept	7,400 units
Oct – Nov	9,300 units

		Cash budget (£)		
Quarter	Opening balance	Receipts	Payments	Closing balance
Jan – Mar	50,000	92,000	86,000	56,000
Apr – Jun	56,000	77,000	75,400	57.600
Jul – Sept	57,600	89,400	91,600	55,400
Oct – Dec	55,400	100,000	97,200	58,200

Here the figures are illustrative only, since the completion of the cash budget requires labour costs, sales revenue, and other details which have been omitted.

8.5.3. Other subsidiary budgets

The *administration budget* is perhaps one of the most simple to prepare, since most administrative costs are independent of the level of manufacturing activity. Similarly, the *research and development (R & D) budget* is not directly related to production. It does, however, present a number of particular difficulties which may be of considerable importance when R and D is a large-scale activity. For instance, heavy investment in specialised staff or equipment over a number of years may be needed, royalties in relation to patents need to be budgeted for, and so on.

The *capital expenditure budget* dovetails with the production budget, and is concerned with plant capacity and the provision of appropriate fixed assets, such as buildings and machinery, in order to provide the necessary facilities to meet planned production.

Finally the *cash budget* – to be prepared by the chief accountant's office – draws together the implications of the earlier budgets by detailing planned receipts and expenditures over the budget period. Opening with the balance at the beginning of this period, all costs of physical and human resources are set against revenues from planned sales. The objective is to ensure the continuing liquidity of the organisation throughout the budget period, and the identification of periods where additional finance might be needed, or where surplus cash might be available for short-term investment.

8.6 The master budget

The *master budget* is a summary of all the individual subsidiary budgets. It is prepared by the budget officer after the budget committee has discussed, and agreed, all the subsidiary budgets. As an overview it will not include, for example, costs of transfer of partially finished goods from one department to another for further processing as these will cancel out. It will,

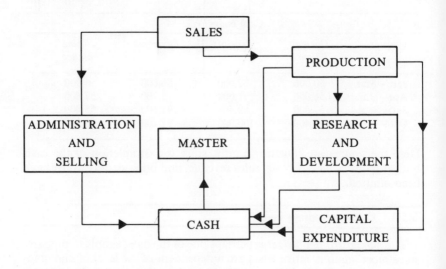

FIG. 29: **Master and main subsidiary budgets**

however, generate a budgeted profit and loss account for the period, and an end-of-period budgeted balance sheet. The master budget is presented by the budget officer, on behalf of the budget committee, to senior management for their approval. Some of the relationships between the more important subsidiary budgets and the master budget are shown in a simplified form in Fig. 29.

8.7 Fixed and flexible budgets

The subsidiary, and therefore the master, budgets are usually designed with a particular level of manufacturing activity in mind. However, it is useful to consider the more realistic situation that, as we progress through the budget period, this planned level of activity may not be achieved. Discrepancies may occur because of unforeseen internal factors (strikes, machine breakdowns, accidents) or external factors (technological innovation by a competitor, changes in economic policy by government). It is not very helpful to have a detailed set of budgets which cannot be modified to meet unforeseen changes in circumstances. The distinction between fixed and variable costs helps us to overcome this practical problem. Fixed costs are, by definition, independent of level of activity – at least over specified ranges of activity level. Variable costs are directly related to activity.

Accordingly, when the budgets are prepared the fixed and variable components of costs for the planned level of activity can be shown separately. If this planned level is not achieved, or is exceeded, it is a simple matter to adjust the budgets:

	Budgeted activity 10,000 DLH	Actual activity 9,000 DLH
Variable costs:		
———— ———— ————	£35,000	£31,500
Fixed costs:		
———— ———— ————	£25,000	£25,000
Total	£60,000	£56,000

With the enormous increase in the use of computers in accounting and financial planning, it is worth noting that the major computer manufacturers offer a wide range of standard programmes, or "software", for use with their machines. These allow the accountant to see very quickly and easily the effects of possible changes in budgeted costs, prices, and production.

8.8 Control

Deviations between actual costs and budget may arise from either external or internal factors. Naturally, it is unlikely that the firm will have any control over the former, but must use the "flex" in its budgets to modify plans accordingly. However, failure to meet budgets due to internal factors may point to a number of things. In the first place, the problem may simply relate to deficiencies in the budgets themselves. Unrealistic targets may have been set which are difficult or impossible to achieve, or inconsistencies may emerge between budgets which had not been appreciated previously. On the other hand, failure to meet budgets may reveal inefficiencies in, for example, manufacturing, purchasing, or in sales. This may indicate the need for counter-measures in order that efficiency may be improved, problems resolved or avoided, and the company's activities placed back on course.

Deviations from budget are revealed to the managers responsible for each budget centre in regular *variance reports*. Often prepared on a monthly basis these show actual costs for the period together with those budgeted. Differences may be *unfavourable* or *adverse* (if actual costs exceed those budgeted, or actual revenues are less than budget), or *favourable* (if actual costs are less than budget, or actual revenues exceed budget).

From the point of view of control, budgeting often goes hand in hand with a *standard costing system*. This is discussed in the next chapter.

Exercises

1. Outline the steps you would take in preparing (i) a labour budget, (ii) a materials budget.

2. "The functions of budgeting are to plan, control, and motivate." Discuss.

3. Explain fully the meaning of "flexible budgeting". Why is an analysis and understanding of cost behaviour essential to the preparation of a flexible budget?

4. Using as an example a small to medium size manufacturing company, prepare a report for management detailing the advantages of a budgetary control system. Provide details of the system you recommend and its operation.

5. Discuss in detail the procedure you would adopt in preparing a sales budget for a new product.

6. Using the following standard cost information, which is based upon sales of 7,500 units during the first quarter of the year:

Sales	115,000
Variable costs:	
Direct materials	25,000
Direct wages	12,000
Overhead	21,000
Fixed costs	32,000
Total cost	90,000
Profit	25,000
Closing stock	Zero

draw up budgets for the next three quarters under (a) absorption costing and (b) marginal costing systems.

The following additional information relates to budgeted production and sales volumes:

Quarter	Production (units)	Sales (units)
2	9,000	6,000
3	7,500	7,500
4	6,000	9,000

Comment on and explain the differences in results using the two systems.

7. The following data concerning Minim Ltd. relate to the month of January:

	Actual	Standard
Output	10,500	9,000
	standard hours	standard hours
	£	£
Direct labour	2,000	2,270
Power	270	287
Indirect materials	330	360
Other variable overhead	1,400	1,800
Fixed overhead	1,000	987

Prepare a flexible budget for the month making, and clearly stating, any necessary assumptions.

8. The following information concerns Maxims Ltd.'s operations over the past three months, and its forecast operations over the next four months:

Month		Sales (£)	Raw materials (£)	Wages (£)	Expenses paid (£)
Jan	(A)	225,000	160,000	42,000	24,000
Feb	(A)	300,000	144,000	63,000	30,000
Mar	(A)	210,000	136,000	56,000	36,000
Apr	(B)	270,000	176,000	49,000	24,000
May	(B)	210,000	128,000	49,000	36,000
June	(B)	225,000	96,000	56,000	30,000
July	(B)	255,000	136,000	49,000	30,000
Aug	(B)	300,000	160,000	56,000	36,000

The figures given for January to March are actual (A), those for April-August are budgeted (B). Prepare a cash budget under an absorption costing system for April-August on the assumption that 60% of cash resulting from sales is received in the month following the sale, and 40% is received in the month after that. Wages are paid one week in arrears, and raw materials are paid for two months after receipt. The bank account has a credit balance of £80,000 at the beginning of April.

Chapter 9

Standard costing

9.1 Introduction

The greater part of this book has been concerned with *actual* or *historic costs*, i.e. costs which have already been incurred. Only in Chapter 5 (when predetermined overhead application rates were developed), and Chapter 8 (when budgeting was discussed) have future costs been introduced. Although of obvious value for purposes of record-keeping and comparison, historic costs are of little use to the manager who is looking to the future.

In the first place, historic costs relate to what has already happened, and do not necessarily convey much information about the future. Manufacturing technology, markets, economic, political and social factors are, after all, continuously changing. Secondly, historic costs alone cannot be judged "good" or "bad" without a standard against which to compare them. The terms "good" and "bad" themselves need making specific. Furthermore, historic costs are of no value from a control point of view: when they are recorded, events have already taken place and it is too late to take any remedial action.

In order to overcome the shortcomings of historic costs from the viewpoint of managerial planning and control, management accountants have developed a system known as *standard costing*. The purpose is to provide an objectively determined structure of costs against which the historic cost structure can be compared. The essential feature of a *standard cost* is that it attaches to a particular operation or part of the manufacturing process an objectively developed cost figure. This is based upon a detailed analysis of the particular operation, and an estimate of the cost which should be incurred by that operation under carefully specified conditions and assumptions. To derive standard costs, a number of different approaches are available. With each approach in general we can also identify three different levels of standard.

9.2 Levels of standard

The *ideal* standard bases costs on the assumption that the organisation always operates at maximum efficiency. It assumes that no labour is lost through sickness, that machines never break down, that materials are

never in short supply, and so on. Such standards are, of course impossible
to meet in practice. Inevitably, actual costs will exceed the ideal. A
disadvantage, therefore, of such a basis for developing standards is that the
labour force is likely to be discouraged by being implicitly asked to strive
for levels of achievement which are unattainable.

Expected standards are produced on the basis of what the organisation is
likely to achieve in its various operations. Although more realistic than the
ideal standard, such a policy nevertheless has a different disadvantage.
Inevitably such standards are related to past performance, and therefore
likely to incorporate past inefficiencies and waste. In other words, this
standard is unlikely to motivate employees to perform any more effectively
and efficiently than they did in the past.

Perhaps the most sensible approach is a policy which identifies *attainable standards*. Such a policy recognises that machine breakdowns and
other production difficulties occur which are outside the control of the
work-force. It aims, nevertheless, at developing standards which can be
attained, but only with considerable effort. From a commonsense viewpoint attainable standards have considerable advantages over either of the
other two. However, actually to produce an agreed set can be exceedingly
difficult, since a balance has to be struck between making them too
difficult to achieve on the one hand, and too easy on the other.

9.3 Derivation of standard costs

Whichever of the three levels of standard suggested in §9.2 is used, we need
to consider now how actual numerical standard cost figures can be
developed.

An obvious way is to look at the past performance of the organisation in
relation to each particular cost. An average figure, or the best figure, over a
number of years could be used. Although relatively simple, this method
does have important disadvantages. Firstly, as we have already noted, past
performance may bear little relationship to the future. Technology, working practices, and skills all change over time. An average figure also suffers
from a lack of incentive. In any case, in setting standards we should have in
mind the future, not the past, since it is with future costs that we are
concerned. This suggests that standards should be based upon forecasts,
for which past costs will not necessarily form a sound basis. With this in
mind let us now turn to three major cost classifications (materials, labour,
and overhead) in more detail.

Machinery and materials have detailed specifications. In the former
these describe what output the machine is capable of providing, and of
what quality for a given input. They also indicate absolute maximum levels
of output, and perhaps maximum sustainable levels. Materials, on the

other hand, are accompanied by specifications with regard to physical properties, purity, content, quality, and so forth. Detailed specifications of this nature can be used to model the operation of the manufacturing process, and to predict quantities and qualities of output under assumed conditions. The purchasing department can provide forecasts of prices of materials based upon knowledge of suppliers and availability of supplies, and from these standard prices are set. Standard quantities and standard unit prices enable standard materials costs to be derived.

Turning now to labour costs, advances in production engineering, time and motion study, and cybernetics over the last few decades provide some basis from which we can analyse worker performance. Complex tasks undertaken by a machinist can, for example, be broken down by the work-study expert into their component parts and standard levels of productivity developed. Such methods can also readily take into account the learning effect which accompanies gradual familiarisation by a worker with a new task (see Chapter 4). Although similarly analytic in nature to the materials standards setting outlined above, these procedures are more difficult to apply in a labour context. Not only do individual workers differ in motivation and ability, but also many may object to the detailed scientific analysis and observation of their work practices.

Finally, standards are needed for overhead expenditure, together with standards for future production capacity in order to develop standard (predetermined) overhead application rates.

To set standards in practice for overhead costs is more difficult than for direct costs. Overhead costs are, after all, less easily identified and therefore less easily analysed objectively. In order to set a standard overhead absorption rate the budgeted overhead costs are divided by a measure of standard production activity. Distinction is usually made between three levels of overall company activity – *ideal*, *attainable*, and *expected* – in exactly the same way as we differentiate between levels of performance at the detailed individual level. *Ideal activity* (*capacity*, *volume*) is the level of production which theoretically could be achieved if the organisation operated always with perfect efficiency. No allowance is made for any deviations from this. *Expected capacity* is that level of production activity needed to meet the expected demand for the company's products over the next year. *Attainable capacity* is the volume of production which could be achieved through continuous operation, but with allowance for holidays, sickness, machine breakdowns and so on. No thought is given to the demand for the company's product in setting attainable capacity.

For most purposes, standard activity is best related to attainable levels, in order to provide the motivation to strive for realistic targets. Usually, production activity is measured in terms of *standard hours*. A standard hour is defined not in terms of time, but in terms of the amount of work which would be performed in a period of one hour at the standard level of activity. It conveniently enables us to measure all production, of perhaps dissimilar items, in the same units.

9.4 Basic variances

The difference between a standard cost and an actual cost is known as the *(cost) variance*. Now, every cost arises as the product of a "quantity" and a "price". Thus, materials costs arise by multiplying a quantity of materials (measured perhaps in litres, kilograms, metres, or simply units) and a price per unit (for example £/kg, or £/metre): labour costs arise from multiplying a quantity (measured usually in labour hours) by a wage rate (£/hour usually). Accordingly, a variance can result from a difference between actual and standard "quantity", actual and standard "price", or both. *Variance analysis* is concerned with the identification and separation of cost variances into components which are themselves the result of materials, labour, or overhead, price or quantity, variances. This description of variance analysis suggests a six-fold classification of variances:

(i) *Materials usage variance* – arising from a difference between actual and standard quantities.

(ii) *Materials price variance* – arising from a difference between actual and standard prices.

(iii) *Labour efficiency variance* – arising from a difference between actual and standard labour hours.

(iv) *Labour rate variance* – arising from a difference between actual and standard wage rates.

(v) *Overhead capacity (or volume) variance* – arising from a difference between budgeted overhead and overhead absorbed.

(vi) *Overhead budget variance* – arising from a difference between actual overhead and budgeted overhead.

Variances are normally designated *favourable* (when actual cost is less than standard) *unfavourable* or *adverse* (when actual cost is greater than standard).

9.5 Materials variances

Perhaps the easiest way of understanding variance analysis is through the use of a diagram (see Fig. 30). Q_A, Q_S denote actual and standard quantities respectively: P_A, P_S denote actual and standard prices.

In this illustration actual quantity (Q_A) exceeds standard quantity (Q_S) by amount EB (i.e. Q_A-Q_S). The materials usage variance is represented by the shaded area FGCH, i.e. $(Q_A$-$Q_S)P_S$. In words:

112 · Standard costing

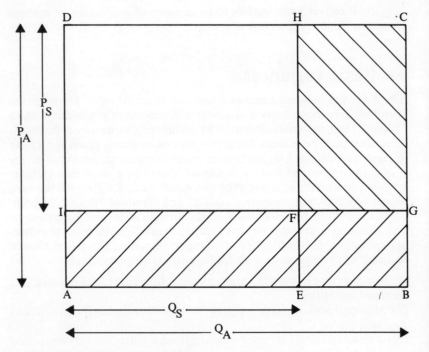

FIG. 30: **Analysis of materials variances**

Materials usage variance = standard price
× difference between actual
and standard quantities.

Similarly, one could define the materials price variance as the product of standard quantity with difference between actual and standard prices, i.e. $(P_A-P_S)Q_S$, or area AEFI. Unfortunately, the effect would be to ignore that part of the cost represented by EBGF, which arises from both differences in actual and standard prices, and differences in actual and standard quantities. Arbitrarily, this cost is normally included as part of materials price variance, which is therefore defined as $(P_A-P_S)Q_A$, or shaded area ABGI. In words:

Materials price variance = actual quantity
× difference between actual
and standard prices.

Having broken down materials cost variance into its two major components the calculations are complete. However, the purpose of the exercise is to highlight potential problems, and an interpretation of any variances is obviously important for purposes of control. It may be, of course, that the standards which have been set are inappropriate and that variances from standard are inevitable. Assuming that this is not the case, however, what meaning can we attach to a materials price variance? Essentially it indicates that the price paid for the materials was not that planned. This may arise, for example, because of unforeseen price rises, because of failure to take advantage of quantity discounts, or because of the need to buy superior quality than originally intended. These possibilities in turn suggest the need perhaps to look for alternative types of raw materials, perhaps to look more carefully at the purchasers' buying policy, or to look for an alternative and more secure source of supply.

A materials usage variance again could arise from a number of causes. Perhaps the wastage rate is higher than expected or the output is lower than planned, suggesting room for improvement by the operators or in their machines. Alternatively, raw materials being used may not be the most suitable, suggesting that purchasing policy needs modifying.

Finally, it is worth emphasising the importance of analysing materials (and, for that matter, labour and overhead) variances into their component parts, since a favourable variance in one might obscure an unfavourable variance in the other. Consider the following:

WORKED EXAMPLE

The standards associated with spraying an area of 4,000m^2 with insecticide are:

Labour time:	1 hour
Labour rate:	£5.50/hour
Materials quantity:	25kg
Materials price:	£0.45/kg

Using these figures, it is estimated that to treat an area of 4 million m^2 will require materials at a cost of:

$$£\frac{4,000,000}{4,000} \times 25 \times 0.45 = £11,250$$

The work is carried out, and actual materials costs turn out to be £11,200. The small favourable (F) materials costs variance is considered insignificant.

Further investigation, however, reveals that the actual materials quantity used was 23,333kg.

Therefore:

Materials usage variance $\quad = £0.45\ (23{,}333 - 25{,}000)$
$$= £750.15\ (F)$$
and Materials price variance $= £23{,}333\ (£\dfrac{11{,}200}{23{,}333} - £0.45)$

$$= £700.15\ (A)$$

The insignificant favourable overall variance is seen to be the combination of two significant variances – one favourable (F) and one unfavourable or adverse (A).

9.6 Labour cost variance

The analysis of labour cost variance follows a similar pattern, illustrated in Fig. 31. Here H_A, H_S represent actual and standard hours worked, and R_A, R_S actual and standard hourly rates. The two component variances are defined by:

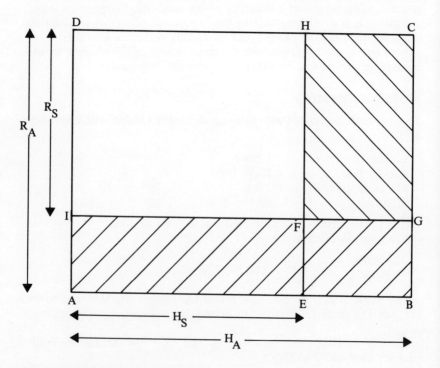

FIG. 31: **Analysis of labour variances**

Labour rate variance = Actual labour hours ×
actual rate – standard rate
$$= H_A (R_A-R_S)$$
i.e. shaded area ABGI

and

Labour efficiency
usage variance = Actual labour hours – standard labour hours ×
standard rate
$$= (H_A-H_S) R_S$$
i.e. shaded area FGCH

Note again the ambiguous nature of cost EBGF which arises from both "price" variances and "quantity" variances. Somewhat arbitrarily it is included in the labour rate variance.

Again, labour rate and efficiency variances may arise from a number of different causes. The former, for example, may be due to an unforeseen new national wage agreement with trades unions, to more or less use of high cost overtime than had been planned, or to the need for more, or less, skilled labour than expected. Efficiency variance may originate from the use of inappropriately skilled labour, bad (or good) supervision, or materials of unexpected quality.

WORKED EXAMPLE

Using the data of §9.5, we have the additional information that labour hours are 970 at a cost of £5,800. Thus:

Labour efficiency usage variance
$$= (970-1,000) × £5.50$$
$$= £165 \text{ (F)}$$

and Labour rate variance

$$= £970 \left(\frac{5,800}{970} - 5.50\right)$$

$$= £465 \text{(A)}$$

9.7 Overhead cost variances

9.7.1 Particular features

Analysis of overhead variances is complicated by a number of factors. In the first place, under an absorption costing system, fixed overhead is allocated to production. Since absorption is based upon a predetermined rate which depends upon a standard activity level and budgeted overhead expenditures, deviations – and therefore cost variances – may originate from either source. Further problems involving labour efficiency also arise when activity is measured in labour hours. In order to clarify the analysis, variable overhead and fixed overhead are treated separately. A full absorption costing system is assumed, and activity is measured, as is usual, in labour hours. We also use the concept of the *standard hour of production*, which is used to measure production in terms of the number of standard hours necessary to achieve that production.

9.7.2 Variable overhead variances

This is defined as the difference between actual variable overhead, AO, (i.e. variable overhead incurred) and variable overhead absorbed. Now, absorption is by a predetermined standard variable overhead application (absorption) rate defined as:

$$\frac{\text{budgeted variable overhead (BO)}}{\text{budgeted standard hours of production (BSH)}}$$

Thus:

$$\text{Variable overhead variance} = \text{AO} - \frac{\text{BO}}{\text{BSH}} \cdot \text{ASH}$$

where ASH is actual standard hours of production, i.e. the standard hours allowed for the level of production actually achieved.

Variances can be seen now to arise from two possible sources:

(i) difference between actual variable overhead and overhead allowed on the basis of hours actually worked, and/or

(ii) difference between actual labour hours and budgeted standard labour hours.

and give rise to the *expenditure variance* and the *efficiency variance* respectively. They are defined as follows where ALH is actual labour hours:

$$\text{Expenditure Variance} = \text{AO} - \frac{\text{BO}}{\text{BSH}} \cdot \text{ALH}$$

$$\text{Efficiency Variance} = \frac{\text{BO}}{\text{BSH}} \cdot \text{ALH} - \frac{\text{BO}}{\text{BSH}} \cdot \text{ASH}$$

The efficiency variance can be interpreted as the difference between variable overhead allowed (on the basis of standard) for the production actually achieved, and the variable overhead applied. The expenditure variance is the difference between actual overhead, and that allowed (on the basis of standard) for production actually achieved. Note that the sum of expenditure and efficiency variances is the total variable overhead variance. Efficiency variance arises from the same sources as the labour efficiency variance, whilst the expenditure variance arises from unexpected changes in indirect labour, materials, and expenses.

WORKED EXAMPLE

Suppose budgeted production is 1,000 units, using 2 standard direct labour hours/unit. Actual production is 950 units, and actual direct labour hours used are 1,800. Actual variable overhead is £11,500. Budgeted variable overhead is £10,000.

Thus:
$$\begin{aligned} AO &= £11,500 \\ BO &= £10,000 \\ ASH &= 1,900 \text{ (i.e. } 950 \times 2) \\ BSH &= 2,000 \text{ (i.e. } 1,000 \times 2) \end{aligned}$$

and therefore,

Variable overhead variance $= £11,500 - (\frac{10,000}{2,000} \times 1,900)$

$$= £2,000 \text{ (A)}$$

In order to analyse this into its components we note that SLH is 1,800. Therefore:

Expenditure variance $= £11,500 - (\frac{10,000}{2,000} \times 1,800)$

$$= £2,500 \text{ (A)}$$

Efficiency variance $= £(\frac{10,000}{2,000} \times 1,800) - (\frac{10,000}{2,000} \times 1,900)$

$$= £500 \text{ (F)}$$

9.7.3 Fixed overhead variances

These are slightly more difficult to analyse. The fixed overhead variance is defined as the difference between actual fixed overhead incurred for the period, and the standard cost of that applied to actual production. Again, absorption is by a predetermined standard fixed overhead application rate defined as:

$$\frac{\text{budgeted fixed overhead (BO)}}{\text{budgeted standard hours of production (BSH)}}$$

Thus:

$$\text{Fixed overhead variance} = AO - \frac{BO}{BSH} \cdot ASH$$

where ASH is the standard hours allowed for production achieved. Note that overhead applied

$$(\text{i.e.} \frac{BO}{BSH} \cdot ASH)$$

is again absorbed here on the basis of standard – not actual – hours for production achieved. The analysis now differs from that of variable overhead, since budgeted fixed overhead does not depend upon activity levels by definition. There is, however, going to be a difference between overhead applied and overhead budgeted unless the achieved activity level is exactly that budgeted. The expression for total variance can be broken down into two components:

$$\text{Fixed overhead variance} = (AO - BO) + (BO - \frac{BO}{BSH} \cdot ASH)$$

$$= \text{budget variance} + \text{volume variance}$$

WORKED EXAMPLE

Extending the previous example, suppose now that actual fixed overhead is £3,000, and budgeted fixed overhead is £3,300. Then:

$$\text{Fixed overhead variance} = £(3,000 - 3,300) + \left(3,300 - \frac{3,300 \times 1,900}{2,000} \right)$$

$$= £135 \text{ (F)}$$

The components are:

Budget variance $= £3,000 - 3,300$
$\qquad\qquad\quad = £300$ (F)
Volume variance $= £165$ (A)

The existence of a budget variance simply indicates that actual fixed overhead costs are different from those which were budgeted. A volume variance arises only when achieved activity differs from that budgeted. If budgeted activity, BSH (measured in standard labour hours) equals achieved activity, ASH (measured in terms of standard hours allowed for production achieved), then:

$$\text{Fixed overhead absorbed} = \frac{BO}{BSH} \cdot ASH$$

$$= \frac{BO}{BSH} \cdot BSH$$

$$= BO$$

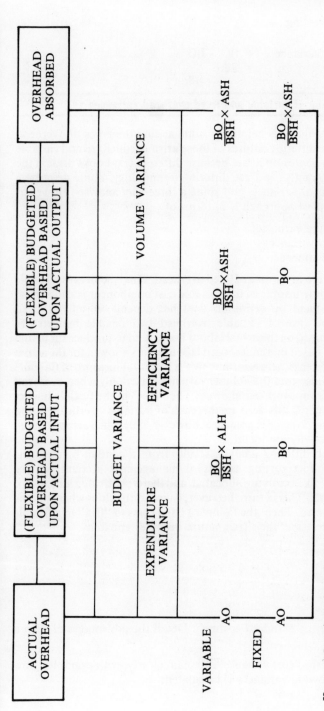

Key: AO = Actual overhead
       BO = Budgeted overhead
       BSH = Budgeted activity (standard hours of production)
       ALH = Actual activity (standard hours allowed for production achieved)
       ALH = Actual activity (actual hours of input)

FIG. 32: Overhead variance analysis

And, volume variance $\quad = BO - BO$
$\qquad\qquad\qquad\qquad = Zero$

9.7.4 Comparison of variable and fixed overhead variances

The schedule of Fig. 32 is helpful in summarising the types of overhead variance, and the differing natures of those arising from fixed and variable overhead. Much confusion arises because different text books present the information differently, and use differing terminology. Some describe a two-way analysis of variance, and some a three-way analysis. However, perhaps the simplest approach is in terms of:

   (i) expenditure variance;
   (ii) efficiency variance;
   (iii) volume variance.

Note that (ii) is zero in the case of fixed overhead. This is so because flexible budgets "flex" only insofar as the variable cost component is concerned: the fixed component by definition does not depend on activity level. However, in the case of variable overhead two flexible budgets are available – one based on the actual labour hours used to produce the actual output, and one based on the standard labour hours allowed for the actual output. The difference between these two is a natural measure of (labour) efficiency. Note also that the volume variance arises only when overhead applied differs from overhead allowed. The "flex" in the flexible budget automatically makes this zero in the case of variable overhead. Fixed overhead volume variance is non-zero, however, only when actual activity and budgeted activity are identical.

Essentially the differing analysis results from a conflict between the control and product costing aspects of management accounting. For product costing, fixed costs are allocated, and therefore treated almost as if they were variable. This in turn, however, causes difficulties when volume is not that budgeted. Then, the failure of fixed costs to "flex" in a flexible budget is revealed, and their true nature becomes apparent.

Exercises

1. Define the term "standard costing". Detail the advantages of such a costing system.

2. Define the term "cost variance". Explain clearly, with examples, how each of the following variances is calculated:

(i) Materials quantity variance;
(ii) Labour rate variance;
(iii) Overhead efficiency variance.

3. Outline the variance analysis of fixed overhead, suggesting the possible origin of each component.

4. "The effectiveness of a standard costing system depends very much on the appropriateness of the standards set." Discuss, with examples.

5. "Cost control is essentially concerned with the identification and reporting of variations between actual and standard. It is management's task then to eliminate the causes of the variations." Discuss.

6. Calculate labour-related variances using the following data:

Standard hours/unit	2.25 hours
Actual hours worked	1,987.5 hours
Standard wage rate	£4.50/hour
Actual wages	£10,080
Actual production	875 units

7. Calculate materials-related variances using the following data:

Standard quantity of raw material/unit	100kg
Standard price of raw material	£78/kg
Actual quantity of raw material/unit	102kg
Actual price of raw materials	£81/kg

8. Using the following data, which relate to a month's operations:

Actual fixed overhead	£2,625
Budgeted fixed overhead	£2,500
Actual number of days worked	20
Budgeted number of days worked	19
Actual hours worked	4,270
Budgeted hours worked	4,090
No. of units produced	4,190
Standard hours/unit	0.95

calculate the fixed overhead variances.

9. For Eagle Enterprises, manufacturers of a single product, use the following information for the month of April to calculate budgeted profit, actual profit, and variances:

	Actual	Budget
Sales (units)	12,000	9,000
Sales price/unit	—	£3.75
Sales values	£48,000	—
Unit manufacturing cost	—	£2.25
Selling and distribution		
Variable	£3,750	£2,250
Fixed	£3,750	£3,000

10. The standard costs associated with manufacturing 750 units of output of a single product are as follows:

		£
Direct materials	7,500kg @ £0.285/kg	2,137.50
Direct labour	375 hours @ £3.80/hour	1,425.00
Overheads:		
Variable	375 hours @ £4.75/hour	1,781.25
Fixed	375 hours @ £2.85/hour	1,068.75
	Total	£6,412.50

In the last 4 weeks actual production was 7,125 units, and budgeted production for that period was 7,500 units. Actual costs were:

		£
Direct materials	(72,000kg)	21,018.75
Direct labour	(3,450 hours)	13,537.50
Overheads:		
Variable		17,100.00
Fixed		11,043.75

Compute all relevant variances and discuss their significance.

11. The following data relate to the overhead costs of Sphinx Industries:

	Actual	Budget
Hours worked	7,800	6,500
Standard hours produced	7,280	—
Variable overhead:		
Power	14,620	12,900
Labour	8,600	10,320
Other	3,440	2,580
Fixed overhead:		
Occupancy	6,020	7,740
Labour	9,460	7,740
Other	5,160	6,020

Analyse the variances.

Chapter 10

Capital budgeting

10.1 Introduction

A manufacturing or service organisation relies normally on the possession of fixed assets to conduct its operations. Such assets include specialised machines, factory sites and buildings, computing facilities, and office equipment. In acquiring fixed assets to use, the organisation is often faced with a choice between several possibilities. A particular task, for example, may be carried out by using a highly specialised machine with low recurrent running costs, but having a large initial purchase price. Alternatively it may be possible to rent such a machine, rather than to purchase it. Yet a third possibility may involve the purchase (or rental) of a less specialised machine with a much lower initial purchase price (or annual rental) and a much higher annual recurrent cost. It is with important financial decisions of this type that the subject of *capital budgeting* (or *capital expenditure analysis*, or *investment appraisal*) is concerned.

The complexity of capital expenditure decisions is largely due to the fact that money does not have a single "value". For example, if offered the choice between receiving £1,000 now, or £1,000 in 20 years' time most people would take the money now. In other words, the same numerical sum of money has a "value" which depends upon time. We now examine this concept in detail.

10.2 The time value of money

10.2.1 Simple interest

Invested money (i.e. *capital*) normally earns *interest*. The interest is paid by the institution or individual in whom the investment is made to the *investor* (i.e. the supplier of the money). It is the "fee" paid to the investor for the use of his money. Always associated with an investment are an *interest rate*, expressed often as a percentage per year, and the *length of time* for which the investment is to run. The total of the initial sum invested (the *principal*) and the interest earned over the *investment period*, is referred to as the *amount*. Consider the following example.

Smith invested £2,000 in a bank for one year at a rate of interest of ten per cent per year (abbreviated to 10% p.a.). At the end of the year the amount of his investment is £2,200:

(P)	Principal:	£2,000
(R)	Interest rate:	10% p.a.
(I)	Interest earned:	£200 (i.e. 10% of £2,000)
(A)	Amount (at year end):	£2,200

More generally the interest, I, earned on an initial investment of P over an investment period of T years, when the interest is 100R% p.a. is given by:

$$I = PTR \qquad\qquad (1)$$

If Smith had invested his money in the bank for two years his interest at the end of the two year period would have been:

$$I = \frac{£2,000 \times 2 \times 10}{100}$$

$$= £400$$

and the amount, A, would have been:

$$\begin{aligned} A &= P + I \\ &= £2,000 + 400 \\ &= £2,400 \end{aligned}$$

Interest earned in this way, and calculated by equation (1) is called *simple interest*.

10.2.2 Compound interest

Normally, interest is not earned on a simple basis, but on a *compound* basis. Under this system interest is added to the principal at regular intervals of time, and the amount used as the principal for the next time period. Again, an example illustrates the process.

Suppose Smith invests £2,000 for two years at an interest rate of 10% p.a. *compounded annually*.

(P_0)	Principal at time 0	: £2,000
	Interest due at time 1	: £200
(P_1)	Amount at time 1	: £2,200
	Principal at time 1	: £2,200
	Interest due at time 2	: £220
(P_2)	Amount at time 2	: £2,420

Note that his compound interest of £420 over the two-year period exceeds his simple interest of £400 by £20. The reason is that under the compound scheme, the £200 interest earned in the first year itself earns interest at a rate of 10% in the second year of the investment period.

In general, under a compound interest scheme the amount, P_1, at the end of year 1 using the above notation is $P_0 + P_0R$, i.e. $P_0 (1 + R)$. At the end of year two the amount is:

$$\begin{aligned} P_1 + P_1R &= P_1 (1 + R) \\ &= P_0 (1 + R) (1 + R) \\ &= P_0 (1 + R)^2 \end{aligned}$$

A simple calculation shows the amount three years after initial investment to be $P_0 (1 + R)^3$, and – in general – after n years to be $P_0 (1 + R)^n$. The factor $(1 + R)^n$ is called the *compounding factor*. For example, if a sum of £900 is invested at 3% p.a. for an investment period of 28 years, the amount at the end of the period is:

$$£900 (1 + 0.03)^{28} = £2,059.11$$

It would obviously be tedious to calculate the compounding factor in the course of each computation of this type. Instead we refer to *compounding tables* (see Appendix A). These provide the appropriate factor for different rates of interest, and different lengths of investment period. Reference to the 3% column and 28 year line reveals that $(1 + 0.03)^{28}$ is 2.2879. Accordingly,

$$\begin{aligned} 900 (1 + 0.03)^{28} &= 900 \times 2.2879 \\ &= 2,059.11 \end{aligned}$$

10.2.3 Present value and discounting

The reverse of the process of compounding interest is known as *discounting*. It can be used when it is necessary to know what principal, P_0, should be invested now, at a given interest rate, in order to have a specified amount A at a chosen date in the future. Given A, the unknown value P_0 is called the *present value* of A. Since, in general

$$A = P_0 (1 + R)^n$$

we know that:

$$P_0 = \frac{A}{(1 + R)^n} = A (1 + R)^{-n}$$

The factor $(1 + R)^{-n}$, is called the *discount factor*. The process of finding P, given values of A, R, and n, is called *discounting*. As in §10.2.2, it would be tedious to calculate the discount factor each time. Instead we can refer to the *discount tables* in Appendix B. Suppose, for example, we want to find the present value of £8,000 due in 20 years' time when the interest rate is 3% p.a. Since

$(1 + 1.03)^{-20} = 0.5537$ we have:
$$P_0 = £8,000 \, (1 + 0.03)^{-20}$$
$$= £8,000 \times 0.5537$$
$$= £4,429.60$$

10.2.4 Equivalence

The sums of money we use in everyday conversation are present values. We talk, for example, of purchasing a new suit or a new dress in terms of how much they will cost now. However, §§10.2.2 and 10.2.3 illustrate that to be precise we must recognise that the timing of the receipt or payment is equally important. This is particularly true in capital budgeting where we are constantly referring to sums of money in the past and future, as well as in the present. We should always refer to the sum of money together with the time at which payment or receipt is made.

The essential idea of the time-value of money is simply stated using the concept of *equivalence*. This states that, when the compound rate is R, the sum of money P – due at a particular date – is *equivalent* to the sum A due n time periods later, if:

$$A = P \, (1 + R)^n$$

A more practical way of looking at equivalence is to say that you are indifferent between having P now, or A, n periods later. This is sensible since by taking P at the given date and investing it at the available rate R, you could collect amount A, n periods later. For example, if the annual rate of interest is 8%, a sum of £20,000 due five years from now is equivalent to £13,611.67 paid now, since

$$£20,000 = £13,611.67 \times (1.08)^5$$

The processes of compounding and discounting convert a sum of money at one date, to an equivalent sum at a later or earlier time respectively. The relationships are illustrated below:

$P \, (1 + R)^{-n}$	P	$P(1 + R)^n$
earlier date	given date	later date

10.2.5 Annuities

An *annuity* is a sequence of payments made at equal intervals of time. The *payment interval* is the time between payments (usually, but not always, a year). The *term* of the annuity is the time from the beginning of the first payment interval to the end of the last. The *present value of an annuity* is the equivalent dated value of the set of payments due at the beginning of the term.

WORKED EXAMPLE

Find the present value, P, of an annuity having six annual payments, each of £200. The discount rate is 5%. The first payment is made one year from the present time.

The schedule of payments is as follows:

	P	£200	200	200	200	200	200
Time	0	1	2	3	4	5	6

The present value of the six payments is not £1,200 (i.e. $6 \times £200$), since this ignores the different time-values of the payments. The first payment at time 1 has a present value of

$\frac{200}{(1.05)}$, the second at time 2 a present value of $\frac{200}{(1.05)^2}$,

and so on. So:

$$P = \frac{200}{1.05} + \frac{200}{(1.05)^2} + \cdots\cdots + \frac{200}{(1.05)^5} + \frac{200}{(1.05)^6}$$

$$= (200 \times 0.9524 + \cdots + (200 \times 0.7462)$$

(using the table in Appendix B).

$$= £200 \times 5.0756$$

$$= £1,015.12$$

Since such calculations occur often it would be tedious to do each in this detailed way. *Annuity tables* (see Appendix C) are available to shorten the calculation. From these we see that for six periods, with a rate of 5% per period, the *annuity factor* is 5.0757. The annuity factor for n periods when the rate is i is written $a_{\overline{n}|i}$ (read "a n angle at i"). It can be shown that:

$$a_{\overline{n}|i} = \frac{1 - (1 + i)^{-n}}{i}$$

Thus, in the above example:

$$a_{\overline{6}|0.05} = \frac{1 - (1.05)^{-6}}{0.05}$$

$$= 5.0757$$

10.2.6 Amortisation

The common process of paying off a debt by equal annual instalments is given the special name of *amortisation*. It is another example of an annuity.

WORKED EXAMPLE

A loan, made now, of £6,000 is to be paid off by four annual equal payments. The interest rate on the amount of the loan unpaid at any time is 12%. Suppose the annual (unknown) repayment is X.

The schedule of payments is therefore:

Repayment	X	X	X	X
Year:	0	1	2	3	4

This forms an annuity. The present value, P, of these payments is therefore:

$$P = \frac{X}{1.12} + \ldots\ldots + \frac{X}{(1.12)^4}$$

$$= 3.0373 \quad \text{(from Appendix C)}$$

The present value of this annuity is equivalent to the present value of the loan, i.e. £6,000. Thus:

$$6,000 = X\,(3.0373)$$
$$\text{i.e. } X = £1,975.44$$

Using the idea of an annuity a complicated calculation has become much simpler. The following table provides a detailed check on the calculation, and an insight into the repayment process

End of year	Interest due at 11%	Annual payment	Principal repaid	Principal remaining unpaid
0	—	—	—	6,000.00
1	720.00	1,975.44	1,255.44	4,744.56
2	569.35	1,975.44	1,406.09	3,338.47
3	400.62	1,975.44	1,574.82	1,763.65
4	211.64	1,975.44	1,763.80	—
Totals	1,901.61	7,901.76	6,000.00	—

The small difference between the final figures of 1,763.65 and 1,763.80 is due to rounding errors.

At the end of the first year the interest bill is £720 (i.e. £6,000 at 12% for one year), and the total debt is therefore £6,720. At that time the first repayment of £1,975.44 is made, and reduces the debt to £4,744.56. This last amount is owed during the second year and at the end of that year the interest owing is £569.35 (i.e. £4,744.56 at 12%). The total debt at the end of the second year is therefore £5,313.91 (i.e. £4,744.56 + £569.35), and at that time the second repayment of £1,975.44 is made. This reduces the debt during the third year to £3,3338.47 (i.e. £5,313.91 – £1,975.44). The process continues in the third and fourth years until the loan and interest are fully repaid.

10.2.7 Sinking funds

A *sinking fund* is created to accumulate a specific sum of money by a specific date. This is done by making regular, equal, payments into an interest-bearing account. It gives yet another illustration of an annuity.

WORKED EXAMPLE

At the end of three years the sum of £8,000 will be needed by a company to pay off some of its loan capital. Money can be invested at a rate of interest of 4% p.a. How much needs to be deposited in a sinking fund at the end of each year in order to accumulate the required sum? Prepare a schedule showing the growth of the fund.

The series of deposits invested, X, is as follows:

Invested		X	X	X
Year	0	1	2	3

The value of the three deposits at time 3 is:

$$X (1.04)^2 + X (1.04) + X$$

and this sum has then to have the value of £8,000. Thus:

$$8,000 = X (1.04)^2 + X (1.04) + 1$$

$$\text{i.e. } X = \frac{8,000}{3.1216}$$

$$= £2,562.79$$

The schedule required is:

End of year	Deposit	Interest on fund	Increase in fund	Amount in fund
1	2,562.79	0	2,562.79	2,562.79
2	2,562.79	102.51	2,665.30	5,228.09
3	2,562.79	209.12	2,771.91	8,000.00
Total	7,688.37	311.63	8,000.00	—

10.3 Uneven cash flows

10.3.1 Net cash inflows and outflows

So far we have looked only at situations where the sequences of payments or receipts – i.e. the *cash flows* – are regular and of equal numerical value. These conditions are necessary to the definition of an annuity. They can really apply, however, only when we have complete control over the schedule of receipts or payments. We now turn to situations where these conditions are not met.

Consider the simplified example of a commercial long-term investment project. It involves the development of a mining site, the extraction of the mineral, the exhaustion of the site, and its closure. The first two years we assume to involve outlays (i.e. expenditures) of capital to develop the site to a point where mining operations can commence. In the following five years net revenues are derived from sales of the extracted mineral. In the last year before closure the seam is exhausted, and the costs of operating are greater than the small revenues derived from sales. The pattern of cash flows might look like this:

End of year	Cash inflow (£000,000)
1	−2.0
2	−1.5
3	+1.0
4	+2.0
5	+3.0
6	+1.5
7	+1.0
8	−3.0

The negative (–) signs indicate that in years 1, 2 and 8 the cash flows were *outflows*, i.e. the company made net payments with regard to the projects. In years 3, 4, 5, 6, and 7 the positive signs indicate that the company had net receipts (or cash *inflows*) from the project as a result of sales of the mineral.

10.3.2 Net present value

We now ask whether there is any way in which a value can be placed upon the *stream of cash flows* in §10.3.1 before the company decides to undertake the project. In other words we assume that we are at time zero, and that we are given the above figures as estimates of future cash flows associated with the project. We are wanting to evaluate the project beforehand.

Simply to add the predicted cash flows together would not be useful, since they occur at different points in time. Money – as we have learned earlier – has a "time-value". In order to combine the cash flows in a sensible way we therefore need an appropriate discount rate. Much has been written concerning the choice of discount rates and it is not possible to explore the issue in detail here. We shall assume a given discount rate, which incorporates inflation, interest rates, and other economic factors, of 10% per annum. We shall also assume for convenience that the cash flows each occur at the end of the year. (In practice sales revenues and capital outlays are likely to take place continuously during the year.) By discounting the expected cash flows back to time zero, and then adding them together, we arrive at a value for the project to the company now. The result is known as the *net present value (NPV)* of the project. In our particular example:

$$ NPV = \frac{(-2.0)}{(1 + 0.10)} + \frac{(-1.5)}{(1 + 0.10)^2} + \frac{(1.0)}{(1 + 0.10)^3} $$
$$ + \ldots + \frac{(1.0)}{(1 + 0.10)^7} + \frac{(-3.0)}{(1 + 0.10)^8} $$

Unfortunately, we cannot use the tables of Appendix C to evaluate this sum since the flows are uneven. However, Appendix B can be used to evaluate the individual terms. Thus:

$$ NVP = (-1.8182) + \ldots + (1.3995) $$
$$ = 0.8827 $$

The result is positive. This shows that the project has a potential benefit to the company. There are many factors involved in the decision whether to invest in a large scale project or not. However, on these figures it looks as though the company should invest in the mining development.

Suppose instead that the cash flow estimates over the eight year period had been as follows:

End of year	Cash inflow (£000,000)
1	−3.0
2	−2.5
3	+0.5
4	+1.5
5	+3.0
6	+1.5
7	+0.5
8	−0.5

The NPV in this case, assuming still a discount rate of 10%, will be:

$$NPV = \frac{(-3.0)}{(1.10)} + \frac{(-2.5)}{(1.10)^2} + \cdots + \frac{(-0.5)}{(1.10)^8}$$

$$= -0.6604$$

Here we see that the net present value of the project to the company is negative. This shows that on the basis of our calculations the company should not invest in the project.

A third possibility would be that a calculation of NPV might, with a particular combination of discount rate and cash flows, be zero. In such a case, using financial criteria alone, the company would be indifferent as to whether it invested in the project or not.

10.3.3 Internal rate of return (IRR)

There is another common approach to the evaluation of a project which, like the method of net present value, also involves discounting. This is known as the *internal rate of return (IRR)* method. Since it is similar to the NPV method, students sometimes find the two confusing. The differences between them lie in the initial assumptions made, and in the questions which each tries to answer. In the case of NPV a value for the discount rate is assumed or given. The question to be answered is: "Does this project have a positive net present value to the company now?" The IRR approach, however, does not assume a discount rate. It asks: "What would the discount rate need to be in order that the company would be indifferent as to whether the project was undertaken or not?" Put slightly differently this latter question asks: "What would the discount rate need to be to make the NPV zero?"

Take the data in §10.3.1: with a discount rate of 10% we calculated an NPV of 0.8827 (£000,000). Suppose now we take a rate of 24%. The NPV would now be −0.0971. Presumably, there is a value of the discount rate somewhere between 10% and 24% for which the NPV is exactly zero. Unfortunately there is no simple way of calculating the value of this discount rate. In effect, we are trying to find a solution for r in the equation:

$$0 = \frac{(-2.0)}{(1 + r)} + \frac{(-1.5)}{(1 + r)^2} + \cdots + \frac{(-3.0)}{(1 + r)^8}$$

and no general method is available other than trial and error. The approximate value is, in fact, r = 22%.

Although the practical interpretation and significance of NPV is fairly simple to understand, IRR is more difficult. A high value of IRR indicates a high *rate of return* to the company on the capital it has invested. Accordingly, the IRR could be interpreted as the highest rate of interest which the company would be prepared to pay on money borrowed for investment in the project. In other words, if this interest rate – or *cost of capital* – in our particular case is greater than 22%, it would not be worth the company's while using borrowed funds to finance investment in the project.

Both IRR and NPV can be used for purposes of comparison. Taking again the expected schedule of cash flows of §10.3.2 we calculate that with an assumed discount rate of 5% the NPV would be positive. The IRR lies therefore in the range 5% – 10%. Successively narrowing the range by trial and error we soon arrive at the value of 6% for the IRR. Comparison of the two series of cashflows in §§10.3.1 and 10.3.2 shows that the company will receive a higher return on its invested capital from the first project. This would be the one to select if a decision had to be made between the two alternatives.

It is not possible in a book of this nature to explore fully the use, the advantages, and the disadvantages of these two methods of investment appraisal. However, a major advantage of the IRR is that it does not rely upon an assumed discount rate. From the decision-maker's point of view, it also gives a convenient basis for comparison with interest rates elsewhere. This is important when considering the costs of sources of funds. It has the disadvantage associated with its calculation (although modern calculators and computing facilities largely remove this problem). It is also possible to identify in some cases more than one possible solution for the IRR, which can make it difficult to interpret. For example, suppose:

Investment at time zero (i.e. now)	£1,000
Cash inflow at end of year one	£2,210
Cash outflow at end of year two	£1,220

The IRR, r, for this project is found as a solution of:

$$0 = -1000 + \frac{2210}{(1 + r)} - \frac{1220}{(1 + r)^2}$$

i.e. r   = 13.7%
   or r =   7.3%

10.4 Other methods of investment appraisal

Particular attention has been given to two methods of capital budgeting which rely on the time-value of money. We turn briefly now to two methods which do not. Although this is a major drawback to the methods they are simple to use. Firstly the *payback period* method asks the question: "How long does it take to recover the initial investment?" Referring once more to §10.3.1, and ignoring the time-value of money, the aggregate cash flows at the end of each year are as follows:

End of year	Aggregate cash flow (£M's)
1	-2.0
2	-3.5 (i.e. -2-1.5)
3	-2.5 (i.e. -2-1.5+1.0)
4	-0.5 (i.e. -2-1.5+1.0+2.0)
5	+2.5 (i.e. -2-1.5+1.0+2.0+3.0)

In this case the payback period is between four and five years. Applying the same procedure to the series of flows in §10.3.2.

End of year	Aggregate cash flow (£M's)
1	-3.0
2	-5.5
3	-5.0
4	-3.5
5	-0.5
6	1.0

Here the payback period is between five and six years. On this criterion the first project would be chosen as superior. The method gives an approximate value for the time which elapses before the initial investment is recovered. However, cash flows after that time are ignored.

The *payback reciprocal* is rather similar. Suppose an initial investment of £20,000 is made, and that the subsequent annual cash inflows are expected to be equal, and of £5,000 each in value. The length of the project is estimated to be ten years. The payback period is in this case four years, and the payback reciprocal is $\frac{1}{4}$, or 25%. It is worth noting that when the total project life is much longer than the payback period, and the cash flows are fairly even, the payback reciprocal is a reasonable approximation to the IRR. Both conditions are satisfied here, and the reader may like to check that the IRR is 22%, and therefore closely approximated by the payback reciprocal of 25%.

Exercises

1. Select the investment which grows to the greatest accumulated sum at the end of its term:

   (a) £1 for 10 periods at 14% compound interest per period;
   (b) £2 for 16 periods at 4% compound interest per period;
   (c) £4 for 1 period at 1% compound interest per period;
   (d) £1 for 32 periods at 5% compound interest per period.

2. Barker invests £400 at 10% per period. Determine the total interest earned on the investment during the eighth and ninth periods (i.e from the end of period seven to the end of period nine).

3. A house sells for £40,000. Purchase is made by a deposit of £4,000 now, with payments of £400 to be made at the end of each month for as long as is necessary. The interest rate is 9% per annum, and is calculated on an annual (not a monthly) basis. How many monthly payments are needed?

4. Mediterranean Fishers are setting up a sinking fund for the purchase of a new boat. They will require £50,000 in five years' time, and can invest at a rate of 5% per annum. What annual deposits must they make? Construct the complete schedule to show the growth of the fund.

5. On his son's fifth birthday a man wishes to deposit with an investment company a sum of money sufficient to provide the boy with a regular yearly income of £1,000 per year for four years, the first coming on his seventeenth birthday. If money can be invested at 6% per annum, what sum should the father deposit?

6. Calculate for the following projects:

	0	1	2	3	4-10	11
Project A	-£12,500	3,500	4,000	4,500	1,000	1,250
Project B	-£12,500	3,500	4,000	4,500	3,000	

(i) The pay-back period;
(ii) The net present value;
(iii) The internal rate of return.

7. Under what circumstances does the pay-back reciprocal provide an approximation to the internal rate of return? Illustrate with appropriate examples.

8. Three independent projects are under consideration by Abacus Ltd. Only one project can be undertaken. The patterns of expected cash flows associated with each are as follows:

	Project		
	I	II	III
Time (years)	£	£	£
0	-80,000	-80,000	-80,000
1	+80,000	+80,000	+16,000
2	+80,000	+75,000	+48,000
3	0	+32,000	+120,000

The company's cost of capital is 10%. Using several different approaches analyse the situation, and comment on your results.

9. Ajax Company purchased a building costing £198,000, of which the company paid £18,000 immediately. The balance was to be paid in equal annual instalments under the terms of a twenty-five year 8% mortgage loan.

Determine the value of the equal instalments to pay off the loan balance over twenty-five years.

Suppose that just after the twelfth payment the company wished to pay off the remaining principal. Determine the principal then outstanding.

10. You are buying a video-recorder with a cash price of £1,100. The salesman informs you that if you pay £98.48 now, the balance can be paid off in twenty-four equal monthly payments of £50 each.

What is the effective annual rate of interest on this purchase contract?

11. A company having a required rate of return of 10% is comparing the following mutually exclusive investment projects. Which would you recommend?

	Initial investment	*Net cash inflows*	
		Year 1	*Year 2*
Project I	£15,000	8,250	14,520
Project II	£30,000	36,000	—

12. Compare and contrast the following approaches to capital expenditure appraisal, drawing attention to the advantages and disadvantages of each:

  (i) Pay-back;
  (ii) Internal rate of return;
  (iii) Net present value.

Chapter 11

Cost analysis for decision making

11.1 Decisions

An essential ingredient of any decision is choice. The person(s) making a decision has to choose between at least two possible alternative *courses of action*. One of these courses of action may be simply to do nothing, as long as a conscious choice has to be made to do nothing, rather than something else. If no choice exists, then no judgement has to be exercised, and no decision can be made: the decision-maker is forced to take the single possible course of action.

In making a choice between alternatives two important aspects of decision-making emerge. Firstly, unless choices are to be made arbitrarily – by tossing a coin, for example – *criteria* for favouring one course of action rather than another have to be established. The most common criterion in a business context is probably *profitability*, i.e. the course of action is chosen which leads to the company generating the maximum profit. However, many other criteria can be suggested: maximisation of shareholder wealth; maximisation of worker satisfaction; maximisation of customer satisfaction; minimisation of environmental damage, are only a few examples. Partly because of the difficulties of measuring values of these, however, choices are usually made on a basis of cost minimisation or profit maximisation.

This brings us to the second major feature of decision-making. Because so many factors affect an organisation's operations it is very difficult to know when, for example, profit is maximised or cost minimised. Recognising this, accountants have introduced the term *satisficing*, which describes performance which is "satisfactory" rather than "best". More importantly, however, decisions are made with the future in mind, and courses of action have to be chosen without knowing for certain what will actually happen. The element of *uncertainty* is inherent in any decision, and the importance of the decision-maker is in exercising judgement in choosing the course of action which will lead to the most satisfactory outcome. It is important to realise that although sophisticated cost analyses, computers, data-banks, and so on may assist the decision-maker, the future remains uncertain. Although the decision-maker has more information, more rapidly available, choices still have to be made between future possibilities with uncertain outcomes. From the viewpoint of the management accountant a number of particular cost concepts have been developed to assist in analysing decisions.

11.2 Costs for decision-taking

11.2.1 Relevant costs

In accounting, the term "relevant" is used in a very specific technical sense, and not in its everyday conversational sense. Its definition is based on the notion that decisions about future actions should be based only on *expected future costs*, and not upon past costs. This is not to say that past costs must be ignored completely. They may be useful in predicting future costs in circumstances which are likely to be similar to those already experienced. What we are saying, however, is that costs should not be considered in making a decision about the future, simply because those costs have been incurred in the past. In a decision-making situation *relevant costs* are those future costs, and only those future costs, which differ between alternative possible courses of future action. Costs which either have occurred in the past, or which do not differ between alternative courses of action, are called *irrelevant costs*.

Consider the simple situation of a young person faced with two possible courses of action with regard to his future career. He may become a full-time student for a number of years, or he may enter full-time employment now. The costs and benefits associated with each course of action are listed below:

Full-time student
Living costs, i.e. food, accommodation
Clothing
Books
Fees
Travel
Grant from education authorities
Expected future salary

Full-time employment
Living costs
Travel
Clothing
Salary (and future prospects)

A comparison of the two lists shows that some items appear in both. In terms of the decision to be made, such items as living costs and clothing are not relevant since they do not differ between the two alternatives. Both costs are incurred whichever course of action is taken. (Of course, it may be that entering full-time employment means that suits, etc., need to be purchased, whereas a student would not need to buy expensive clothing. Any difference of this nature would be a relevant cost.) In looking at income, which appears on both lists, the person needs to find the differences between his expected flows of salary over many years into the future, and the relatively low income he received as a student for a few years, but which presumably is followed by much greater salaries in future years as a result of his better education. In proceeding down the two lists, it is always the differences in future costs and benefits which are relevant. Costs and benefits which are the same whichever course of action is taken are irrelevant.

11.2.2 Sunk costs

Following the distinction between future and past costs comes the concept of *sunk costs*. These are historical costs (i.e. costs already incurred) which are the result of a past decision and which cannot be recovered through a future decision. As such they cannot be affected by a future decision, and in our specialised sense of the word, they are irrelevant. Care needs to be taken in using the term sunk cost. For example, suppose a new machine has just been bought at a cost of £100,000, when suddenly a different, superior, machine becomes available for purchase. As a result, it is decided that the second machine would be more suitable for the company's needs, and therefore the machine which has just been bought should not be used. The whole of the £100,000 is not a sunk cost, since by selling the machine some of the cost can be recovered. If it can be sold for £80,000, then only the remaining £20,000 represents a sunk cost.

11.2.3 Opportunity costs

Since a decision involves the choice of one course of action from at least two possibilities, it is obvious that in making the decision at least one possible course of action must be abandoned, or foregone. In foregoing an alternative we are sacrificing possible benefits that might have resulted had we chosen that alternative. In this context the monetary benefits that would have resulted from the course of action foregone are referred to as *opportunity costs*.

As a simple illustration, suppose a firm had the choice between two alternative investments A and B. The latter has a net present value of £2M.

The opportunity costs of choosing to invest in A rather than B is therefore £2M.

11.2.4 Differential costs

The concept of a *differential cost* overlaps a little with that of a relevant cost. The former, however, arises in situations where we are considering various possible levels of production output, and is defined as the difference in total costs arising from two different output levels. Clearly, variable costs – by definition – will form part of the differential costs. Additionally, however, there may typically be a component which arises from the need to provide additional manufacturing capacity in the form of plant and machinery.

11.2.5 Out-of-pocket costs

This rather odd term is used to refer to costs, short-term in nature – which arise as a result of a particular decision. For example, if a special order, additional to normal production, is accepted the costs of extra raw materials and labour could be classed as out-of-pocket costs.

11.2.6 Avoidable costs

Finally, in our brief discussion of special decision-making costs we introduce the idea of an *avoidable cost*. The term is used with reference to costs which will not be incurred if a particular course of action is not taken. Quite simply, for example, if the decision was taken not to introduce the manufacture of a new product, the materials, labour, and other costs associated with that new product would be avoidable costs.

11.3 Decision-making in practice

11.3.1 Introduction

In the remainder of this chapter we shall look at a number of specific decision situations in which some of the categories of cost introduced above will be used. In doing so, however, it is worth noting that the classifications overlap: an out-of-pocket cost may also be an avoidable cost, a relevant cost may be a differential cost, and so on. The names are intended simply to help the decision-maker in his analysis, they are not intended to be unique and rigid classifications.

11.3.2 Special orders

A simple illustration of the relevant cost concept relates to the decision whether to meet certain sales demands or not. It also uses the distinction between direct and absorption costing, which was discussed at length in Chapter 6.

Consider the following situation

Production volume	200,000 units
Fixed overhead	£150,000
Unit costs:	
Direct materials	£1.25
Direct labour	£1.75
Variable overhead	£0.50
Total variable costs/unit	£3.50
Fixed overhead/unit	£0.75
Total cost/unit	£4.25

Current selling price is £4.60/unit.

The company, which has the finished goods available in stock, now receives an offer from a retailer to buy 50,000 units at £3.80/unit. Should the company accept the offer or not?

One argument would be that the total cost of manufacture is £4.25 per unit and, since the potential buyer is offering less than that figure, that the order should not be accepted. Such an argument would suggest that to accept the order would involve a loss to the manufacturer of 50,000×£0.45, i.e. £22,500.

However, such an argument fails to recognise the relevant costs in the situation. Firstly, we need to identify possible future situations, of which there are many. At one extreme there may be no further demand for the 50,000 units, and the manufacturer may be left with stock of increasing obsolescence, and decreasing sales value. Alternatively, he may envisage a buoyant demand for the products and therefore a constant stream of alternative sales outlets. Whatever scenario he thinks the most likely, the only strictly relevant consideration is the future sales revenue. All fixed overhead costs and variable costs are sunk costs, and therefore irrelevant. The decision can be analysed therefore in the following terms:

(a) Accept order:
Sales revenue = 50,000 × £3.80
= £190,000
(b) Reject order:
Sales revenue lies between 0 and £230,000.

Without the experience of the marketing/sales staff it is not possible to proceed further, since the likelihood of realising a sales figure in (b), which exceeds that of (a), is not known.

11.3.3 Additional production volume

The decision situation of $11.3.2 can be given a different perspective if the special order comes for units additional to the 200,000 already produced, and for which a market has already been determined. We use the same basic figures:

Production volume	200,000 units
Fixed overhead	£150,000
Unit costs:	
Direct materials	£1.25
Direct labour	£1.75
Variable overhead	£0.50
Total variable cost/unit	£3.50
Fixed overhead/unit	£0.75
Total cost/unit	£4.25

Current selling price is £4.60/unit.

The order is now for 50,000 more units (for which production capacity is assumed to exist without hiring additional staff, purchasing new machinery, etc.). The market for the existing 200,000 @ £4.60 is assumed certain. Two alternatives exist, but the relevant costs are different from those in §11.3.2:

(a) *Accept additional order*

Incremental sales	50,000 × £3.80 = £190,000
Incremental (or differential)	
costs	50,000 × £3.50 = £175,000
Incremental net income	£15,000

(b) *Reject additional order*

Incremental net income	Zero

Looked at in this analytical fashion it is clear that (a) is the preferred course of action. Note that only the variable production costs are relevant, and that the fixed costs – which are incurred whether the additional order is accepted or not – are not relevant. This argument would imply, of course, that any additional sales demand at a price in excess of £3.50/unit should be met. Obviously, although this would be strictly logical, there are other considerations which would need to be taken into account if many orders of this nature were to be received. For instance, the present capacity of the plant would soon be exceeded, other regular customers would begin to ask why the prices they were paying were in excess of that of the customers who placed "special orders", and would themselves seek price reductions. The principle upon which the decision has been justified in this example is one of marginal costing, and will remain valid only for marginally extra orders.

11.3.4 Limiting factors of production

A fairly common manufacturing decision concerns the choice between different product lines. Again, this can raise some interesting cost considerations, one of which is illustrated by the following.

Suppose a manufacturer is wishing to launch a new product, of which there are three possible variants, with differing cost structures as follows:

	Variant I	Variant II	Variant III
Selling price/unit	£30.00	£22.50	£12.00
Variable cost/unit	£18.00	£11.00	£9.00
Marginal contribution/ unit	£12.00	£11.50	£3.00

At first sight one might feel that Variant I had a slight advantage over Variant II, and that both had considerable advantages over Variant III in terms of the contribution each is likely to make to overall company profits. However, the schedule above gives only part of the information important to the decision. Given the same pattern of fixed costs whichever variant is chosen, the variants differ in the manufacturing times associated with each:

Hours to complete one unit	$3\frac{1}{2}$	4	$\frac{3}{4}$
Marginal contribution to profits per unit	£3.43	£2.87	£4.00

This puts a different complexion on the decision and suggests that Variant III might be the best one to produce. The altered view arises from recognising that – if plenty of material and labour are available, together with a ready market – time is the major constraint, and therefore that in a working day it is preferable to make more of the cheapest product when the objective is profit maximisation.

The point here is that a limiting factor – which in this case is time, but could in other contexts be the availability of labour or raw materials – can have a crucial impact on the decision.

11.3.5 Make or buy decisions

A manufacturing company may well be faced with the decision whether to make components itself, or to buy ready-made components from an outside supplier. The decision obviously has meaning only in situations where excess capacity exists within the company, or when additional capacity can be made available by the purchase of additional resources. In the first case the decision is likely to hinge on marginal cost considerations, whilst in the latter the incremental costs associated with the provision of further capacity are also introduced.

Furthermore, the devotion of resources to making a component will inevitably raise the question of opportunity costs foregone by not using those resources in some alternative way.

Consider a case where over the next month budgeted capacity is 9,000 direct labour hours, whilst normal capacity is 10,000. Each unit requires $\frac{1}{3}$ direct labour hours in its manufacture. Direct labour costs £3/hour. The materials cost to make a component A is £2/unit. Incremental indirect manufacturing costs are £2,000. The need is for 3,000 units of A.

To manufacture these the costs will be:

Materials	£6,000
Direct labour	£3,000
Indirect manufacturing costs	£2,000
Total	£11,000
Cost/unit	£3,668

If, therefore, an outside supplier can provide the components at a unit cost less than £3.67 the company would be advised to purchase rather than make them itself. We have ignored the possible deployment of expected excess labour hours in some other aspect of the company's activities. If such an alternative use exists we would need to take account of the opportunity costs associated with it.

11.3.6 Opportunity costs

It was explained earlier that opportunity costs arise in relation to an alternative course of action which is not taken. An opportunity cost is a benefit foregone by the decision-maker in choosing one from several courses of action. Suppose a tradesman owns two small shops which he currently operates for himself. The shops contain fixtures and fittings, and in order to run his trading operations he needs to maintain levels of inventory (stocks) in each premises. He receives from another tradesman an offer to lease one or both of the premises for a period of five years. The decision confronting our tradesmen is whether to continue operating the premises himself, or to lease them to the other man. The costs involved are as follows:

Net income	Shop A	£8,000 per annum
	Shop B	£8,800 per annum
Lease offers	Shop A	£6,000 per annum
	Shop B	£4,800 per annum

Present investment in each shop:

Shop A	Inventory (annual average)	£28,000
	Fixtures and fittings	£5,600
Shop B	Inventory	£8,000
	Fixtures and fittings	£1,400

Suppose he were to continue operating both shops. The rental payments foregone would then be opportunity costs, as would the interest (assumed to be 10%) which he could otherwise earn on the capital now invested in inventory and fixtures. A full comparison of his costs would take the form:

		Shop A		*Shop B*
Income		8,000		8,800
less opportunity costs				
(a) Rental	6,000		4,800	
(b) Interest	3,360	9,360	940	5,740
	Net	(£1,360)		£3,060

He would be advised therefore to rent out Shop A, and to continue operating B.

It might be useful to analyse the problem from the viewpoint of adopting the second course of action in which case the roles of the costs are reversed. Thus:

		Shop A		*Shop B*
Income (i) Rental	6,000		4,800	
(ii) Interest	3,360	9,360	940	5,740
less opportunity cost		8,000		8,800
(i.e. income from trading)	Net	£1,360		£(3,060)

The outcome of the decision, of course, remains unchanged.

11.3.7 Replacement decisions

As a final illustration, we turn to the analysis of replacement decisions. Typically, the organisation needs to decide whether old plant or equipment, with perhaps increasingly high running costs, should be replaced by more expensive new assets with greater reliability perhaps, and lower recurrent maintenance costs. Such decisions are made by individuals when, for example, choosing between running an old car (involving small capital investment but high maintenance costs), or buying a newer vehicle (with a larger capital outlay but less maintenance).

Consider the following detailed example:

	Old machine	New machine
Original purchase price	£9,000	£8,500
Age (years)	4	—
Total life	10	6
Present scrap value	£1,000	—
Scrap value at end of life	£300	£350
Annual operating costs	£15,000	£13,000
Present (depreciated) book value	£5,400	—

A simple (but incorrect) approach would be to argue as follows:

Costs of investment in new machine:	
Purchase cost	£8,500
Loss on old machine (£5,400 less £1,000)	£4,400
Total	£12,900

Savings in operating costs (over next 6 years of useful life @ £2,000 per year)	£12,000

Using this faulty analysis we would conclude that the old machine should be retained, since the savings in operating costs are less, by £900, than the capital costs.

The major flaw in this argument is its incorporation of the book value of the old machine. This value is of use only in an accounting sense, and is derived from the application of mechanical accounting conventions only. Its numerical value is related to the original purchase price in a convenient, but arbitrary, way. In any case, the purchase price of this machine four years ago is a sunk cost with no relevance to the current decision.

Assuming that both machines are equally effective, giving equal quantity and quality of outputs for equal inputs, a cash flow analysis based upon relevant costs would proceed as follows:

	Continue with old machine	Purchase new machine	Difference
Purchase cost of new machine	—	8,500	−8,500
Operating costs over next 6 years	90,000	78,000	12,000
Scrap value of old machine now	—	−1,000	1,000
Scrap value of old machine in 6 years' time	−300	—	−300
Scrap value of new machine in 6 years' time	—	−350	350
Net difference			£4,550

Other costs, all of which are either not in the future, or do not differ between alternatives, are not relevant to the decision. The conclusion therefore is that the old machine should be replaced by the new one.

Exercises

1. Indicate, with reasons, which of the following factors need to be taken into account in the decision whether to buy a new machine or not:

   (i) Cost of installing new machine is £350;
  (ii) Additional investment in current assets of £8,000 will be needed;
 (iii) The old machine has a scrap value of £7,000;
 (iv) The old machine has a book value of £5,500;
  (v) The book gain on sale of the old machine is £1,500.

2. Ultra Ltd.'s profits are thought to be too low. The company is offered a large contract at a price somewhat below current production costs. Describe the circumstances under which Ultra might be wise to accept the contract.

3. Panacea Ltd. has a contribution margin ratio of 60%. It is estimated that one out of four of the orders received by Panacea from customers with a poor credit rating will result in a bad debt.

   Currently 20 of these orders await processing: each is for £150. The credit controller has decided to refuse these orders since in his view a probable loss of £750 from £3,000 is too great. In fact past records indicate that losses from bad debts amount to no more than $\frac{1}{3}$% of sales.

   Comment in detail on his decision.

4. Trinkets Ltd. manufacture fashion goods. It is considering purchasing a new machine to manufacture a bauble having a maximum selling life of sixteen months. The cost of the machine is £3,750, including installation charges. Since the machine – which has a life of three years – can be used for no other purpose than manufacturing baubles, it has a scrap value of only £250. A maintenance contract will need to be taken out on acquisition of the machine, at a cost of £525. Without the machine labour costs of manufacture would be £375 per month, but using the machine these would reduce to £125 per month.

By analysing appropriate cash flows justify clearly your recommendation to purchase the machine or not.

5. Emptor Ltd. owns the machinery necessary to make a small component used in one of its own finished products. This machinery, which cost £25,500 and has a scrap value now of £3,500, cannot be used for any other purpose. Its present book-value is £14,000, and it has zero scrap value in three years' time at the end of its life. If the machinery is not put into use now it will be scrapped immediately. If it is put into use additional factory space will need to be rented at a cost of £7,700 per annum. The following are the expected production costs:

	Per unit
Direct material	£4.90
Direct labour	2.10
Fixed overhead	1.40
Variable overhead	2.10
Depreciation	1.75

Production, which is expected to be at a level of 2,000 components per year, would be over the next three years only. Stocks of raw materials, having an average value of £2,100 would need to be maintained throughout the period. Emptor's cost of capital is 11%.

Recommend to Emptor whether it should make the component itself, or buy from an outside supplier at a guaranteed price of £14 per component.

6. Ravan Ltd. wishes to tender for a contract to supply the Veneguayan Government with school desks. The contract is for 4,250 desks per month, and Ravan produce now similar desks which sell at £19 each.

The following information is available:

	Actual costs last month (25,500 units produced)	Budgeted costs at normal capacity (34,000 units)
Direct materials	£89,250	£119,000
Direct labour	76,500	102,000

	Actual costs last month (25,500 units produced)	Budgeted costs at normal capacity (34,000 units)
Indirect labour	51,000	68,000
Power	26,350	34,000
Depreciation	25,500	25,500
Maintenance	21,250	21,250
Factory supervision	46,750	59,500
Distribution	17,850	23,800
Sales commissions	20,400	27,200
Advertising	18,700	22,100
Administration	20,400	20,400

What is the minimum price per desk which Ravan can offer to the Veneguayan Government?

Chapter 12

Epilogue

In Chapter 1 attention was drawn to the major roles of management accounting in planning, decision-making, and control. The point was also made that in order to fulfil these roles the management accountant needs to draw upon many other disciplines. As we have seen, these include the behavioural sciences, statistics, management science/operational research, and computing/information science. Unfortunately, in an introductory text such as this it is impossible to explore all aspects of the subject of management accounting fully. Inevitably choices have to be made with regard to topic emphasis and topic range. In conclusion, however, it may be of interest and value to the reader to give a brief overview of current issues, recent developments, and aspects of the subject which have been given only scant treatment.

Perhaps because they had been previously neglected, the behavioural aspects of management accounting are those to which the greatest attention has been directed in recent years. Although at its most fundamental level management accounting is concerned with the processing of internal financial information, this information is then used by people. The manner in which people – either individually or in groups – respond to information is therefore of crucial importance if planning, control, and decision-making are to take place in a manner consistent with attainment of company objectives. As a very simple example, it is common practice for department heads in a budgeting context to overstate expected expenditures in anticipation of budgets being reduced by a budget committee. In the same context, participation in budget-setting is a recognition that employees may be better motivated to meet a budget which they are able to influence themselves. Again, accounting information can be used to provide measures of company (financial) performance. More particularly, such information can be used within a divisionalised company to provide comparative performance measures of individual managers. Few managers, however, would be motivated to perform better using measures based upon some factors over which they had little or no personal control (fixed assets, for example).

A major difficulty in advancing our understanding in this area is the complexity of human behaviour. Not only is it difficult to describe objectivity or unambiguously, but it is also difficult to "measure" and therefore to predict.

Less controversial, but again only introduced briefly in this book, is the part played in management accounting by mathematical and statistical models. These tend to fall into two categories: the deterministic and the stochastic. The former assume that numerical quantities have certain values. Thus, given definite figures for future marginal profits on each of a range of manufactured products, together with numerical constraints on supplies of labour, raw materials, and other physical resources involved in manufacture, the well-established techniques of linear programming will provide unambiguous figures for the numbers of units to be produced in order to maximise profit. Stochastic models on the other hand introduce the more realistic assumption that future values of costs, sales, and so on are not known with certainty but follow probability distributions. The complexity of this latter type of model has largely been overcome by the use of computer simulations. In essence, the approach is to examine the effects on the model of a range of, say, possible costs and prices. The speed of computer operations enables this to be done very readily in a manner which was previously not practicable. Many computer programs are now available which enable the accountant to examine a range of possible scenarios in the contexts of, for example, inventory control, budgeting, and cash management.

Finally, mention must be made of developments in information technology. Modern microprocessor technology has meant that vast amounts of information not only on the organisation itself, but also on external markets, on competitors, and on national and international factors can be made available very cheaply and very rapidly. The implications for speedy, more effective and better informed decision-making, and for planning, feed-back and control are very far-reaching. However, there is also the danger that so much information can obscure that which is vital amongst that which is less relevant, and can pose major problems of security. The full impact of the "information technology revolution" will take many years to absorb. There is little doubt that for the accountant and his profession, those years will present both challenge and opportunity.

Appendix A

Compounding factors

Period	1%	2%	3%	4%	5%	6%	7%	8%	9%	10%
1	1.0100	1.0200	1.0300	1.0400	1.0500	1.0600	1.0700	1.0800	1.0900	1.1000
2	1.0201	1.0404	1.0609	1.0816	1.1025	1.1236	1.1449	1.1664	1.1881	1.2100
3	1.0303	1.0612	1.0927	1.1249	1.1576	1.1910	1.2250	1.2597	1.2950	1.3310
4	1.0406	1.0824	1.1255	1.1699	1.2155	1.2625	1.3108	1.3605	1.4116	1.4641
5	1.0510	1.1041	1.1593	1.2167	1.2763	1.3382	1.4026	1.4693	1.5386	1.6105
6	1.0615	1.1262	1.1941	1.2653	1.3401	1.4185	1.5007	1.5869	1.6771	1.7716
7	1.0721	1.1487	1.2299	1.3159	1.4071	1.5036	1.6058	1.7138	1.8280	1.9487
8	1.0829	1.1717	1.2668	1.3686	1.4775	1.5938	1.7182	1.8509	1.9926	2.1436
9	1.0937	1.1951	1.3048	1.4233	1.5513	1.6895	1.8385	1.9990	2.1719	2.3579
10	1.1046	1.2190	1.3439	1.4802	1.6289	1.7908	1.9672	2.1589	2.3674	2.5937
11	1.1157	1.2434	1.3842	1.5395	1.7103	1.8963	2.1049	2.3316	2.5804	2.8531
12	1.1268	1.2682	1.4258	1.6010	1.7959	2.0122	2.2522	2.5182	2.8127	3.1384
13	1.1381	1.2936	1.4685	1.6651	1.8856	2.1329	2.4098	2.7196	3.0658	3.4523
14	1.1495	1.3195	1.5126	1.7317	1.9799	2.2609	2.5785	2.9372	3.3417	3.7975
15	1.1610	1.3459	1.5580	1.8009	2.0789	2.3966	2.7590	3.1722	3.6425	4.1772
16	1.1726	1.3728	1.6047	1.8730	2.1829	2.5404	2.9522	3.4259	3.9703	4.5950
17	1.1843	1.4002	1.6528	1.9479	2.2920	2.6928	3.1588	3.7000	4.3276	5.0545
18	1.1961	1.4282	1.7024	2.0258	2.4066	2.8543	3.3799	3.9960	4.7171	5.5599
19	1.2081	1.4568	1.7535	2.1068	2.5270	3.0256	3.6165	4.3157	5.1417	6.1159
20	1.2202	1.4859	1.8061	2.1911	2.6533	3.2071	3.8697	4.6610	5.6044	6.7275
21	1.2324	1.5157	1.8603	2.2788	2.7860	3.3996	4.1406	5.0338	6.1088	7.4002
22	1.2447	1.5460	1.9161	2.3699	2.9253	3.6035	4.4304	5.4365	6.6586	8.1403
23	1.2572	1.5769	1.9736	2.4647	3.0715	3.8197	4.7405	5.8715	7.2579	8.9543
24	1.2697	1.6084	2.0328	2.5633	3.2251	4.0489	5.0724	6.3412	7.9111	9.8497
25	1.2824	1.6406	2.0938	2.6658	3.3864	4.2919	5.4274	6.8485	8.6231	10.835
26	1.2953	1.6734	2.1566	2.7725	3.5557	4.5494	5.8074	7.3964	9.3992	11.918
27	1.3082	1.7069	2.2213	2.8834	3.7335	4.8223	6.2139	7.9881	10.245	13.110
28	1.3213	1.7410	2.2879	2.9987	3.9201	5.1117	6.6488	8.6271	11.167	14.421
29	1.3345	1.7758	2.3566	3.1187	4.1161	5.4184	7.1143	9.3173	12.172	15.863
30	1.3478	1.8114	2.4273	3.2434	4.3219	5.7435	7.6123	10.063	13.268	17.449
40	1.4889	2.2080	3.2620	4.8010	7.0400	10.286	14.974	21.725	31.409	45.259
50	1.6446	2.6916	4.3839	7.1067	11.467	18.420	29.457	46.902	74.358	117.39
60	1.8167	3.2810	5.8916	10.520	18.679	32.988	57.946	101.26	176.03	304.48

Future value of £1 at the end of n periods: $(1 + i)^n$

Period	12%	14%	15%	16%	18%	20%	24%	28%	32%	36%
1	1.1200	1.1400	1.1500	1.1600	1.1800	1.2000	1.2400	1.2800	1.3200	1.3600
2	1.2544	1.2996	1.3225	1.3456	1.3924	1.4400	1.5376	1.6384	1.7424	1.8496
3	1.4049	1.4815	1.5209	1.5609	1.6430	1.7280	1.9066	2.0972	2.3000	2.5155
4	1.5735	1.6890	1.7490	1.8106	1.9388	2.0736	2.3642	2.6844	3.0360	3.4210
5	1.7623	1.9254	2.0114	2.1003	2.2878	2.4883	2.9316	3.4360	4.0075	4.6526
6	1.9738	2.1950	2.3131	2.4364	2.6996	2.9860	3.6352	4.3980	5.2899	6.3275
7	2.2107	2.5023	2.6600	2.8262	3.1855	3.5832	4.5077	5.6295	6.9826	8.6054
8	2.4760	2.8526	3.0590	3.2784	3.7589	4.2998	5.5895	7.2058	9.2170	11.703
9	2.7731	3.2519	3.5179	3.8030	4.4355	5.1598	6.9310	9.2234	12.166	15.917
10	3.1058	3.7072	4.0456	4.4114	5.2338	6.1917	8.5944	11.806	16.060	21.647
11	3.4785	4.2262	4.6524	5.1173	6.1759	7.4301	10.657	15.112	21.199	29.439
12	3.8960	4.8179	5.3503	5.9360	7.2876	8.9161	13.215	19.343	27.983	40.037
13	4.3635	5.4924	6.1528	6.8858	8.5994	10.699	16.386	24.759	36.937	54.451
14	4.8871	6.2613	7.0757	7.9875	10.147	12.839	20.319	31.691	48.759	74.053
15	5.4736	7.1379	8.1371	9.2655	11.974	15.407	25.196	40.565	64.359	100.71
16	6.1304	8.1372	9.3576	10.748	14.129	18.488	31.243	51.923	84.954	136.97
17	6.8660	9.2765	10.761	12.468	16.672	22.186	38.741	66.461	112.14	186.28
18	7.6900	10.575	12.375	14.463	19.673	26.623	48.039	85.071	148.02	253.34
19	8.6128	12.056	14.232	16.777	23.214	31.948	59.568	108.89	195.39	344.54
20	9.6463	13.743	16.367	19.461	27.393	38.338	73.864	139.38	257.92	468.57
21	10.804	15.668	18.822	22.574	32.324	46.005	91.592	178.41	340.45	637.26
22	12.100	17.861	21.645	26.186	38.142	55.206	113.57	228.36	449.39	866.67
23	13.552	20.362	24.891	30.376	45.008	66.247	140.83	292.30	593.20	1178.7
24	15.179	23.212	28.625	35.236	53.109	79.497	174.63	374.14	783.02	1603.0
25	17.000	26.462	32.919	40.874	62.669	95.396	216.54	478.90	1033.6	2180.1
26	19.040	30.167	37.857	47.414	73.949	114.48	268.51	613.00	1364.3	2964.9
27	21.325	34.390	43.535	55.000	87.260	137.37	332.95	784.64	1800.9	4032.3
28	23.884	39.204	50.066	63.800	102.97	164.84	412.86	1004.3	2377.2	5483.9
29	26.750	44.693	57.575	74.009	121.50	197.81	511.95	1285.6	3137.9	7458.1
30	29.960	50.950	66.212	85.850	143.37	237.38	634.82	1645.5	4142.1	10143.
40	93.051	188.88	267.86	378.72	750.38	1469.8	5455.9	19427.	66521.	·
50	289.00	700.23	1083.7	1670.7	3927.4	9100.4	46890.	·	·	·
60	897.60	2595.9	4384.0	7370.2	20555.	56348.	·	·	·	·

Appendix B

Discounting factors

Number of periods	1%	2%	3%	4%	5%	6%	7%	8%	9%	10%
1	.9901	.9804	.9709	.9615	.9524	.9434	.9346	.9259	.9174	.9091
2	.9803	.9612	.9426	.9246	.9070	.8900	.8734	.8573	.8417	.8264
3	.9706	.9423	.9151	.8890	.8638	.8396	.8163	.7938	.7722	.7513
4	.9610	.9238	.8885	.8548	.8227	.7921	.7629	.7350	.7084	.6830
5	.9515	.9057	.8626	.8219	.7835	.7473	.7130	.6806	.6499	.6209
6	.9420	.8880	.8375	.7903	.7462	.7050	.6663	.6302	.5963	.5645
7	.9327	.8706	.8131	.7599	.7107	.6651	.6227	.5835	.5470	.5132
8	.9235	.8535	.7894	.7307	.6768	.6274	.5820	.5403	.5019	.4665
9	.9143	.8368	.7664	.7026	.6446	.5919	.5439	.5002	.4604	.4241
10	.9053	.8203	.7441	.6756	.6139	.5584	.5083	.4632	.4224	.3855
11	.8963	.8043	.7224	.6496	.5847	.5268	.4751	.4289	.3875	.3505
12	.8874	.7885	.7014	.6246	.5568	.4970	.4440	.3971	.3555	.3186
13	.8787	.7730	.6810	.6006	.5303	.4688	.4150	.3677	.3262	.2897
14	.8700	.7579	.6611	.5775	.5051	.4423	.3878	.3405	.2992	.2633
15	.8613	.7430	.6419	.5553	.4810	.4173	.3624	.3152	.2745	.2394
16	.8528	.7284	.6232	.5339	.4581	.3936	.3387	.2919	.2519	.2176
17	.8444	.7142	.6050	.5134	.4363	.3714	.3166	.2703	.2311	.1978
18	.8360	.7002	.5874	.4936	.4155	.3503	.2959	.2502	.2120	.1799
19	.8277	.6864	.5703	.4746	.3957	.3305	.2765	.2317	.1945	.1635
20	.8195	.6730	.5537	.4564	.3769	.3118	.2584	.2145	.1784	.1486
21	.8114	.6598	.5375	.4388	.3589	.2942	.2415	.1987	.1637	.1351
22	.8034	.6468	.5219	.4220	.3418	.2775	.2257	.1839	.1502	.1228
23	.7954	.6342	.5067	.4057	.3256	.2618	.2109	.1703	.1378	.1117
24	.7876	.6217	.4919	.3901	.3101	.2470	.1971	.1577	.1264	.1015
25	.7798	.6095	.4776	.3751	.2953	.2330	.1842	.1460	.1160	.0923
26	.7720	.5976	.4637	.3607	.2812	.2198	.1722	.1352	.1064	.0839
27	.7644	.5859	.4502	.3468	.2678	.2074	.1609	.1252	.0976	.0763
28	.7568	.5744	.4371	.3335	.2551	.1956	.1504	.1159	.0895	.0693
29	.7493	.5631	.4243	.3207	.2429	.1846	.1406	.1073	.0822	.0630
30	.7419	.5521	.4120	.3083	.2314	.1741	.1314	.0994	.0754	.0573
35	.7059	.5000	.3554	.2534	.1813	.1301	.0937	.0676	.0490	.0356
40	.6717	.4529	.3066	.2083	.1420	.0972	.0668	.0460	.0318	.0221
45	.6391	.4102	.2644	.1712	.1113	.0727	.0476	.0313	.0207	.0137
50	.6080	.3715	.2281	.1407	.0872	.0543	.0339	.0213	.0134	.0085
55	.5785	.3365	.1968	.1157	.0683	.0406	.0242	.0145	.0087	.0053

Present value of £1: $1/(1 + i)^n$

Number of periods	12%	14%	15%	16%	18%	20%	24%	28%	32%	36%
1	.8929	.8772	.8696	.8621	.8475	.8333	.8065	.7813	.7576	.7353
2	.7972	.7695	.7561	.7432	.7182	.6944	.6504	.6104	.5739	.5407
3	.7118	.6750	.6575	.6407	.6086	.5787	.5245	.4768	.4348	.3975
4	.6355	.5921	.5718	.5523	.5158	.4823	.4230	.3725	.3294	.2923
5	.5674	.5194	.4972	.4761	.4371	.4019	.3411	.2910	.2495	.2149
6	.5066	.4556	.4323	.4104	.3704	.3349	.2751	.2274	.1890	.1580
7	.4523	.3996	.3759	.3538	.3139	.2791	.2218	.1776	.1432	.1162
8	.4039	.3506	.3269	.3050	.2660	.2326	.1789	.1388	.1085	.0854
9	.3606	.3075	.2843	.2630	.2255	.1938	.1443	.1084	.0822	.0628
10	.3220	.2697	.2472	.2267	.1911	.1615	.1164	.0847	.0623	.0462
11	.2875	.2366	.2149	.1954	.1619	.1346	.0938	.0662	.0472	.0340
12	.2567	.2076	.1869	.1685	.1372	.1122	.0757	.0517	.0357	.0250
13	.2292	.1821	.1625	.1452	.1163	.0935	.0610	.0404	.0271	.0184
14	.2046	.1597	.1413	.1252	.0985	.0779	.0492	.0316	.0205	.0135
15	.1827	.1401	.1229	.1079	.0835	.0649	.0397	.0247	.0155	.0099
16	.1631	.1229	.1069	.0930	.0708	.0541	.0320	.0193	.0118	.0073
17	.1456	.1078	.0929	.0802	.0600	.0451	.0258	.0150	.0089	.0054
18	.1300	.0946	.0808	.0691	.0508	.0376	.0208	.0118	.0068	.0039
19	.1161	.0829	.0703	.0596	.0431	.0313	.0168	.0092	.0051	.0029
20	.1037	.0728	.0611	.0514	.0365	.0261	.0135	.0072	.0039	.0021
21	.0926	.0638	.0531	.0443	.0309	.0217	.0109	.0056	.0029	.0016
22	.0826	.0560	.0462	.0382	.0262	.0181	.0088	.0044	.0022	.0012
23	.0738	.0491	.0402	.0329	.0222	.0151	.0071	.0034	.0017	.0008
24	.0659	.0431	.0349	.0284	.0188	.0126	.0057	.0027	.0013	.0006
25	.0588	.0378	.0304	.0245	.0160	.0105	.0046	.0021	.0010	.0005
26	.0525	.0331	.0264	.0211	.0135	.0087	.0037	.0016	.0007	.0003
27	.0469	.0291	.0230	.0182	.0115	.0073	.0030	.0013	.0006	.0002
28	.0419	.0255	.0200	.0157	.0097	.0061	.0024	.0010	.0004	.0002
29	.0374	.0224	.0174	.0135	.0082	.0051	.0020	.0008	.0003	.0001
30	.0334	.0196	.0151	.0116	.0070	.0042	.0016	.0006	.0002	.0001
35	.0189	.0102	.0075	.0055	.0030	.0017	.0005	.0002	.0001	·
40	.0107	.0053	.0037	.0026	.0013	.0007	.0002	.0001	·	·
45	.0061	.0027	.0019	.0013	.0006	.0003	.0001	·	·	·
50	.0035	.0014	.0009	.0006	.0003	.0001	·	·	·	·
55	.0020	.0007	.0005	.0003	.0001	·	·	·	·	·

Appendix C

Present value of an annuity of £1 per period for n periods, $a_{\overline{n}|i}$

Number of Periods	1%	2%	3%	4%	5%	6%	7%	8%	9%
1	0.9901	0.9804	0.9709	0.9615	0.9524	0.9434	0.9346	0.9259	0.9174
2	1.9704	1.9416	1.9135	1.8861	1.8594	1.8334	1.8080	1.7833	1.7591
3	2.9410	2.8839	2.8286	2.7751	2.7232	2.6730	2.6243	2.5771	2.5313
4	3.9020	3.8077	3.7171	3.6299	3.5460	3.4651	3.3872	3.3121	3.2397
5	4.8534	4.7135	4.5797	4.4518	4.3295	4.2124	4.1002	3.9927	3.8897
6	5.7955	5.6014	5.4172	5.2421	5.0757	4.9173	4.7665	4.6229	4.4859
7	6.7282	6.4720	6.2303	6.0021	5.7864	5.5824	5.3893	5.2064	5.0330
8	7.6517	7.3255	7.0197	6.7327	6.4632	6.2098	5.9713	5.7466	5.5348
9	8.5660	8.1622	7.7861	7.4353	7.1078	6.8017	6.5152	6.2469	5.9952
10	9.4713	8.9826	8.5302	8.1109	7.7217	7.3601	7.0236	6.7101	6.4177
11	10.3676	9.7868	9.2526	8.7605	8.3064	7.8869	7.4967	7.1390	6.8052
12	11.2551	10.5753	9.9540	9.3851	8.8633	8.3838	7.9427	7.5361	7.1607
13	12.1337	11.3484	10.6350	9.9856	9.3936	8.8527	8.3577	7.9038	7.4869
14	13.0037	12.1062	11.2961	10.5631	9.8986	9.2950	8.7455	8.2442	7.7862
15	13.8651	12.8493	11.9379	11.1184	10.3797	9.7122	9.1079	8.5595	8.0607
16	14.7179	13.5777	12.5611	11.6523	10.8378	10.1059	9.4466	8.8514	8.3126
17	15.5623	14.2919	13.1661	12.1657	11.2741	10.4773	9.7632	9.1216	8.5436
18	16.3983	14.9920	13.7535	12.6593	11.6896	10.8276	10.0591	9.3719	8.7556
19	17.2260	15.6785	14.3238	13.1339	12.0853	11.1581	10.3356	9.6036	8.9501
20	18.0456	16.3514	14.8775	13.5903	12.4622	11.4699	10.5940	9.8181	9.1285
21	18.8570	17.0112	15.4150	14.0292	12.8212	11.7641	10.8355	10.0168	9.2922
22	19.6604	17.6580	15.9369	14.4511	13.1630	12.0416	11.0612	10.2007	9.4424
23	20.4558	18.2922	16.4436	14.8568	13.4886	12.3034	11.2722	10.3711	9.5802
24	21.2434	18.9139	16.9355	15.2470	13.7986	12.5504	11.4693	10.5288	9.7066
25	22.0232	19.5235	17.4131	15.6221	14.0939	12.7834	11.6536	10.6748	9.8226
26	22.7952	10.1210	17.8768	15.9828	14.3752	13.0032	11.8258	10.8100	9.9290
27	23.5596	20.7069	18.3270	16.3296	14.6430	13.2105	11.9867	10.9352	10.0266
28	24.3164	21.2813	18.7641	16.6631	14.8981	13.4062	12.1371	11.0511	10.1161
29	25.0658	21.8444	19.1885	16.9837	15.1411	13.5907	12.2777	11.1584	10.1983
30	25.8077	22.3965	19.6004	17.2920	15.2725	13.7648	12.4090	11.2578	10.2737
35	29.4086	24.9986	21.4872	18.6646	16.3742	14.4982	12.9477	11.6546	10.5668
40	32.8347	27.3555	23.1148	19.7928	17.1591	15.0463	13.3317	11.9246	10.7574
45	36.0945	29.4902	24.5187	20.7200	17.7741	15.4558	13.6055	12.1084	10.8812
50	39.1961	31.4236	25.7298	21.4822	18.2559	15.7619	13.8007	12.2335	10.9617
55	42.1472	33.1748	26.7744	22.1086	18.6335	15.9905	13.9399	12.3186	11.0140

10%	12%	14%	15%	16%	18%	20%	24%	28%	32%
0.9091	0.8929	0.8772	0.8696	0.8621	0.8475	0.8333	0.8965	0.7813	0.7576
1.7355	1.6901	1.6467	1.6257	1.6052	1.5656	1.5278	1.4568	1.3916	1.3315
2.4869	2.4018	2.3216	2.2832	2.2459	2.1743	2.1065	1.9813	1.8684	1.7663
3.1699	3.0373	2.9137	2.8550	2.7982	2.6901	2.5887	2.4043	2.2410	2.0957
3.7908	3.6048	3.4331	3.3522	3.2743	3.1272	2.9906	2.7454	2.5320	2.3452
4.3553	4.1114	3.8887	3.7845	3.6847	3.4976	3.3255	3.0205	2.7594	2.5342
4.8684	4.5638	4.2883	4.1604	4.0386	3.8115	3.6046	3.2423	2.9370	2.6775
5.3349	4.9676	4.6389	4.4873	4.3436	4.0776	3.8372	3.4212	3.0758	2.7860
5.7590	5.3282	4.9464	4.7716	4.6065	4.3030	4.0310	3.5655	3.1842	2.8681
6.1446	5.6502	5.2161	5.0188	4.8332	4.4941	4.1925	3.6819	3.2689	2.9304
6.4951	5.9377	5.4527	5.2337	5.0286	4.6560	4.3271	3.7757	3.3351	2.9776
6.8137	6.1944	5.6603	5.4206	5.1971	4.7932	4.4392	3.8514	3.3868	3.0133
7.1034	6.4235	5.8424	5.5831	5.3423	4.9095	4.5327	3.9124	3.4272	3.0404
7.3667	6.6282	6.0021	5.7245	5.4675	5.0081	4.6106	3.9616	3.4587	3.0609
7.6061	6.8109	6.1422	5.8474	5.5755	5.0916	4.6755	4.0013	3.4834	3.0764
7.8237	6.9740	6.2651	5.9542	5.6685	5.1624	4.7296	4.0333	3.5026	3.0882
8.0216	7.1196	6.3729	6.0472	5.7487	5.2223	4.7746	4.0591	3.5177	3.0971
8.2014	7.2497	6.4674	6.1280	5.8178	5.2732	4.8122	4.0799	3.5294	3.1039
8.3649	7.3658	6.5504	6.1982	5.8775	5.3162	4.8435	4.0967	3.5386	3.1090
8.5136	7.4694	6.6231	6.2593	5.9288	5.3527	4.8696	4.1103	3.5458	3.1129
8.6487	7.5620	6.6870	6.3125	5.9731	5.3837	4.8913	4.1212	3.5514	3.1158
8.7715	7.6446	6.7429	6.3857	6.0113	5.4099	4.9094	4.1300	3.5558	3.1180
8.8832	7.7184	6.7921	6.3988	6.0442	5.4321	4.9245	4.1371	3.5592	3.1197
8.9847	7.7843	6.8351	6.4338	6.0726	5.4509	4.9371	4.1428	3.5619	3.1210
9.0770	7.8431	6.8729	6.4641	6.0971	5.4669	4.9476	4.1474	3.5640	3.1220
9.1609	7.8957	6.9061	6.4906	6.1182	5.4804	4.9563	4.1511	3.5656	3.1227
9.2372	7.9426	6.9352	6.5135	6.1364	5.4919	4.9636	4.1542	3.5669	3.1233
9.3066	7.9844	6.9607	6.5335	6.1520	5.5016	4.9697	4.1566	3.5679	3.1237
9.3696	8.0218	6.9830	6.5509	6.1656	5.5098	4.9747	4.1585	3.5687	3.1240
9.4269	8.0552	7.0027	6.5660	6.1772	5.5168	4.9789	4.1601	3.5693	3.1242
9.6442	8.1755	7.0700	6.6166	6.2153	5.5386	4.9915	4.1644	3.5708	3.1248
9.7791	8.2438	7.1050	6.6418	6.2335	5.5482	4.9966	4.1659	3.5712	3.1250
9.8628	8.2825	7.1232	6.6543	6.2421	5.5523	4.9986	4.1664	3.5714	3.1250
9.9148	8.3045	7.1327	6.6605	6.2463	5.5541	4.9995	4.1666	3.5714	3.1250
9.9471	8.3170	7.1376	6.6636	6.2482	5.5549	4.9998	4.1666	3.5714	3.1250

Index

The Author of this Handbook

JOHN P. DICKINSON is Professor of Accounting and Director of Postgraduate Studies, University of Glasgow. He has held university posts in Leeds, Lancaster, Western Australia, Dundee and Stirling. He is the author of four other books and also of very many articles in learned journals. He is a former Chairman and Managing Director of a publishing company, and Director of Credit Union. He has had both teaching and management experience in the UK and overseas in areas of management accounting, business finance and quantitative analysis, and has had experience of consultancy assignments in various organisations. He is an adviser to several overseas educational institutions on the development of accounting and management education.